Dec., 1990

Dear Dad,
    Enjoy!
HAPPY Holidays!
    LOVE,
        Jenifer

LAKE COUNTY

O H I O

LAKE COUNTY

O H I O

150 YEARS OF TRADITION

Bari Oyler Stith

"PARTNERS IN PROGRESS" BY IRENE CHANG

PRODUCED IN COOPERATION WITH
THE LAKE COUNTY HISTORICAL SOCIETY

WINDSOR PUBLICATIONS, INC.
NORTHRIDGE, CALIFORNIA

Frontispiece: The promise of a new life awaited pioneers in Lake County. This painting, done by an unknown artist circa 1825, portrayed the peaceful life waiting along the Grand River in Painesville. The view was probably painted from the perspective of the Main Street Bridge. Courtesy, Lake County Historical Society

Windsor Publications, Inc.—History Book Division

Vice-President/Publishing: Hal Silverman
Editorial Director: Teri Davis Greenberg
Corporate Biographies Director: Karen Story
Design Director: Alexander D'Anca

Staff for *Lake County, Ohio: 150 Years of Tradition*
Editor: Marilyn Horn
Photo Editor: Laura Cordova
Assistant Editor: Jeff Reeves
Assistant Director, Corporate Biographies: Phyllis Fockler Gray
Editor, Corporate Biographies: Judith L. Hunter
Layout Artist, Corporate Biographies: Mari Catherine Preimesberger
Editorial Assistants: Didier Beauvoir, Thelma Fleischer, Alyson Gould, Kim Kievman, Michael Nugwynne, Kathy B. Peyser, Pat Pittman, Theresa Solis
Proofreader: Susan J. Muhler
Sales Representative, Corporate Biographies: Jack Hurt
Layout Artist, Editorial: Robaire Ream
Designer: Ellen Ifrah

Library of Congress Data—
Stith, Bari.
Lake County, Ohio: 150 years of tradition/Bari Oyler Stith. p. 9 cm.
"Partners in progress by Irene Chang."
"Produced in cooperation with the Lake County Historical Society."
Bibliography: p. 122
Includes index.
ISBN 0-89781-249-2
1. Lake County (Ohio)—History. 2. Lake County (Ohio)—Description and travel—Views. 3. Lake County (Ohio)-—Industries. I. Lake County Historical Society. II. Title.
F497.L2S57 1988
977.1'334—dc19 87-34090 CIP

CONTENTS

PREFACE

HIGHLY IMPORTANT!
GREAT INDIGNATION MEETING AT
PAINESVILLE

Under these headlines the battle for the creation of Lake County finally hit the front page of the Painesville *Telegraph* on March 10, 1840. The struggle was not a new one. Painesville citizens had petitioned the Ohio General Assembly for the creation of a new county in October 1839, and *Telegraph* editor L.L. Rice had dutifully reported the progress of that application in his regularly published notes on the proceedings of the Ohio Legislature. Usually appearing on pages two and three of the then-weekly newspaper, this item's placement on page one indicated that the issue was considered crucial, having already been defeated once and then revived for reconsideration. The newspaper announcement invited "men of all [political] parties . . . to consider whether any and what further measures are necessary to be taken to promote the passage of the bill."

Ten days later, the Ohio General Assembly established the new County of Lake by consolidating Willoughby Township of Cuyahoga County and the seven northernmost townships of Geauga County. The *Telegraph* resumed its usual pattern of reporting the news with front-page headlines focused on state and national politics and international events such as the royal wedding of Britain's Albert and Victoria. Lake Countians continued on as before, the excitement of the new county fading into memory under the pressures of everyday life. But boundaries had been created and, although they were invisible on the physical landscape, they repre-

sented a choice made by the people of eight different townships to separate from the counties to which they had belonged for three decades and band together in a new community. That choice would prove not only long lasting, but worthy of celebration in 1990.

From the vantage point of more than a century, tradition emerges as a central theme in Lake County's history. The ties binding Lake Countians to their original New England roots have been intertwined with the innovations required for life in a new territory and the tradition of each wave of immigrants, whether they came from as far away as Eastern Europe at the turn of the century or as close as Cleveland in the 1980s. And this heritage has been enriched by peoples of the prehistoric past and the uplift, struggle, and change that sculptured our landscape long before the arrival of humankind on the Western Reserve horizon.

With lawns overlooking Lake Erie, the Shore Club developed into a popular vacation spot from 1898 to 1921. Its large, two-story clubhouse with its wide porches served as a focus for social events. Courtesy, Lake County Historical Society

7

W.L. TAYLOR.

Two women accompanied the 1796 surveying party to the Western Reserve. Anna Gun remained in Conneaut with her husband Elijah, who took charge of the commissary cabin there, and Tabitha Cumi Stiles aided her husband Job as he supervised the company's supplies at Cleveland. Both women wintered in the Reserve with their husbands. This engraving of the landing of the surveying party was done by W.L. Taylor and appeared in Harvey Rice's *Pioneers of the Western Reserve* in 1888.

FROM THE DAWN OF TIME

Over 15,000 years ago the last of the glaciers, the Wisconsin, crept

across Ohio, advancing and then retreating as it redefined the phys-

ical landscape. Life fled before an onslaught that sheared off moun-

taintops to fill neighboring valleys and left in its wake hills of debris

and a layer of fine topsoil. Within a few thousand years it stretched

as far south as the Cincinnati area in the western portion of the state and Columbiana County in the east. Then it began a rapid retreat until, by about 12,300 B.C., the glacier covered only the far northern part of Ohio. Today, although the Wisconsin glacier is only a memory, its effect is visible in places like Stebbin's Gulch at Holden Arboretum, where the stream bed cuts through geologic time.

Over the next 6,000 years modern Lake Erie and its river drainages were established and, as the Ohio climate warmed, flora and fauna developed in profusion. The higher elevations of the land boasted an abundance of pine and hemlock, and the virgin white pine standing today on the summit of Little Mountain may be the last of its kind in Ohio. On the lower elevations, deciduous forests of maple, hickory, black walnut, chestnut, and oak flourished with an undergrowth that included witch hazel, huckleberry, and trailing arbutus. Predators such as black bears, wolves, and panthers roamed the forests along with the elk and the deer. Beavers were especially plentiful, creating their own ponds by damming the rushing streams and natural springs.

This was prehistoric Ohio, a land shared between animals such as the giant beaver and the mastodon, and Paleo-Indians, who may

The budding peach trees of the Cole Nurseries, shown here early in the century, were the result of a combination of the county's favorable climate and fertile soil, which developed by about 6,000 B.C. Courtesy, Lake County Historical Society

have wandered the glaciated portions of the state as early as 11,500 B.C. These peoples seem to have vanished by about 8,000 B.C., either through migration northward or by merging with the Archaic People.

The hunting and gathering lifestyle of the Archaic period carried over into the Woodland Indian period which followed it after 1,500 B.C. These later peoples, generally termed the Adenas and the Hopewells, were somewhat less nomadic. The Adenas may have been one of the first early hunting groups to experiment with the cultivation of produce such as pumpkins and squash. But despite the importance of their first farming efforts, these Woodland Indians are probably best remembered for their burial practices, which earned them the name of Mound Builders. This term is often used generically, as it is here, for a variety of early cultures that had similar burial practices but may otherwise have been unrelated. Although the Adena and Hopewell peoples are linked through their mortuary practices and their simultaneous occupation of the Ohio territory from about 700 B.C. to 300 B.C., it was the Hopewells who excelled in constructing complex systems of earthworks through the use of various geometric shapes and low, rounded mounds. Such complexity may have been encouraged by advances in food production, which may have afforded artists and shamans more time for their creations.

While the Adena and Hopewell cultures are considered representative of the climax of mound building in the Ohio territory, they were not the last practitioners of this type of burial. After their decline several other prehistoric groups developed, including those of the Whittlesey Focus whose residence in northern Ohio has been dated from A.D. 900 to 1650.

Little Mountain features attributed to glaciation include large boulders placed along the mountain slopes, as if a giant hand had heaved them indiscriminately over the landscape, and deep, narrow chasms and crevices cut in eerie formations through the Sharon conglomerate. This picture was reproduced from a stereopticon view taken by H. Eggleston in the 1870s. Courtesy, Lake County Historical Society

Although only partially excavated, the Kerniskey site has yielded shell and bone remains, ceramic vessels, tools, pipes, and a few graves. The artifacts pictured here are bird bones, otolith, and elk canine teeth which have been found since 1980 in the Lake County excavations. Courtesy, Case Western Reserve University

The people of the Whittlesey Focus clustered around the central shore of Lake Erie and were named after Colonel Charles Whittles of Cleveland who, during the nineteenth century, described many of their archaeological sites. The Native peoples' extended occupation of this area reveals the gradual changes wrought by the introduction of new crops and agricultural styles, exposure to other cultures through increased trade, and population increases which resulted in the enlargement of villages. In addition to this long-ranging mural of prehistoric time, ongoing archaeological excavations are also revealing slices of everyday life which indicate that the Whittlesey people relied partially on primitive forms of agriculture. They used stone tools and ceramic vessels, lived in oval houses often located near waterways, and buried their dead in shallow graves, sometimes near their homes and sometimes in nearby cemeteries.

These people have often been linked with the Erie Indians who were reportedly destroyed in 1654 by the bold Iroquois of the New York region. Mystery shrouds the Erie because of their lack of written history and their lack of contact with the early European explorers of the Great Lakes. Much of our knowledge comes from the *Jesuit Relations,* writings of the French Jesuit priests who may never have actually come into contact with the Erie and wrote from information gathered from other Indian tribes.

Today archaeologists and historians alike question the linkage between the Whittlesey peoples who inhabited the southern Lake

Part of our knowledge about the Erie Indians comes from colonial maps, which were often compiled from second- and third-hand accounts of Indians, explorers, and sometimes royal cartographers who never left the court to view the land they were drawing. By 1755 when Lewis Evans prepared this map, the Erie Nation was no longer included on such maps. From *Early History of Cleveland,* 1867

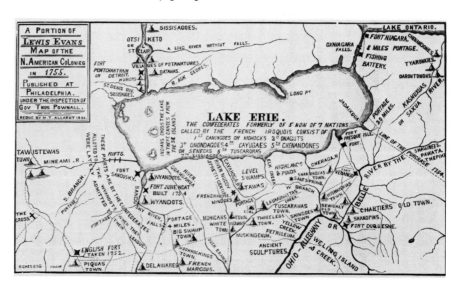

Erie shore and the Erie Indians who have been identified as occupying the Niagara Frontier region at the eastern end of the lake. This discussion is not necessarily new but has been energetically renewed over the past decade, in part because of the archaeological excavations currently in progress in Lake County.

Of the approximately 250 archaeological sites which have been identified in Lake County, only a few have been excavated. Although some of the mounds have been obliterated during the construction of roads and buildings, several excavations have been performed during the twentieth century. The earliest were the 1929 excavations at the junction of Paine Creek and Grand River in Leroy, at Mill Creek and Grand River in Madison, and on Reeve Road near Lake Shore Boulevard in Eastlake. Less than 10 years later, Richard Morgan and Robert Goslin of the Ohio State Museum, Harding High School principal Elijah Brown, and several students excavated a site in Fairport Harbor. Since 1980 archaeologists in the Western Reserve have pursued the study of the county's prehistoric past with digs at the Kerniskey site in Eastlake and the Norma Grantham site in Fairport Harbor. Both sites were uncovered by the landowners and have been identified as the Whittlesey Focus of the late Woodland period. Under the direction of Professor David R. Bush, director of the Archaeology Laboratory at Case Western Reserve University, these excavations are yielding surprising results that provide information for new discussions and may eventually change our local legends.

While the Kerniskey site in Eastlake is significant in its status as one of the few remaining village sites of the Whittlesey period, the Norma Grantham site in Fairport Harbor is important for the number of human skeletal remains which have been uncovered. Discoveries such as these may eventually allow archaeologists to project life expectancies and the standards for family relationships that these people experienced. How many living parents and grandparents could a child expect to have when he reached his tenth birthday? How long could he expect to live? How would he die—through natural causes, an arrowhead from a warring tribe, or through his lack of immunity to the European diseases which were introduced

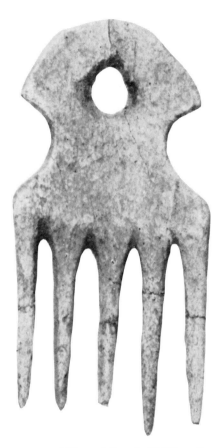

This comb from the Whittlesey Focus was found during the recent excavation of two archaeological sites in Lake County. Since 1980, digs at the Kerniskey site in Eastlake and the Norma Grantham site in Fairport Harbor have yielded surprising results. Courtesy, Case Western Reserve University

The Norma Grantham site in Fairport Harbor appears to have been a cemetery for a nearby village. Archaeologists suspect links between it and the Fairport Harbor Village site excavated in the 1930s. Both mass and single graves have been found. This single grave was uncovered in 1985. Courtesy, Case Western Reserve University

in the Americas during the seventeenth century? Both sites are significant for what they reveal about the region before and after the introduction of European culture.

In the seventeenth century the Indians of the entire Great Lakes region felt the impact of the Europeans who were also attracted to the area, the French being the first. Although historians disagree as to whether or not Robert Cavalier, Sieur de la Salle, passed through northern Ohio on his return from Illinois during the 1680s, it is known that Louis Jolliet had made a map of Lake Erie for La Salle in 1669 and that Abbe Rene de Brehant de Galinee and Dollier de Casson, members of La Salle's expedition, later separated from the main party to lead a group of fellow Sulpician missionaries to the Detroit River. On this trip they were forced to establish a winter camp on the south shore of Lake Erie several days west of the Grand River. Although improbable, local legend locates this camp at the mouth of the Chagrin River, then called the Biche by the French.

As the century progressed French *coureurs de bois* explored this virgin territory in search of prime pelts, particularly beaver, and often resided with the Indians until trading posts and forts could be established on both Lake Erie and the Ohio River. Some local historians claim that by mid-century a small post called Charlton was operating at the mouth of the Biche River.

The extension of these French posts from the Canadian provinces into Ohio encouraged the return of Indian tribes such as the Ottawas, Wyandots, and Chippewas from the north. In the eighteenth century Ohio came alive with peaceful Indian activity which continued until competition between the French and the English escalated into hostility.

Endeavors to control the rich territory of the Ohio Country despite the Indian occupation and the rivalry in the fur trade have been credited as chief causes of the French and Indian War, which began in 1754. Despite the fact that many Indian tribes aided the French, considering them less of a threat to their own interests, the English formally claimed victory in 1763, although they had received the French possessions in Canada three years earlier.

At that time Major Robert Rogers and his Rangers were sent into the Lake Shore region to claim the French forts on Lake Erie and in the West. It was during this expedition that the Rangers met with a delegation of Pontiac's Ottawas at the mouth of either the Grand or the Cuyahoga River to discuss their journey westward. In

Early European explorers of the Great Lakes region included French trappers and Jesuit priests such as Father Pere Marquette. The Jesuit *Relations*, annual reports sent to France by the New World missionaries, record that in the mid-eighteenth century the French had established a trading post called Charlton at the mouth of the Biche River (known today as the Chagrin). This engraving of Father Marquette appeared in J.S.C. Abbott's *The History of the State of Ohio* in 1875

1760 the British forces were given permission to continue; three years later the Ottawa chief was less cordial in his relations with his European neighbors. His spring attack on Detroit encouraged a series of Indian uprisings among the tribes occupying the fringes of settlement from the Great Lakes to the Virginia backcountry.

Gradually treaties and military expeditions forced the Indians to surrender their title to the lands south of the lake and east of the Cuyahoga River. Their final defeat occurred at the Battle of Fallen Timbers. The resulting Treaty of Greenville in 1795 provided the opening of part of Ohio and a generous strip of eastern Indiana to white settlement. This drastically changed the pattern of migration, for after 1795 settlement in groups for mutual protection was no longer necessary and pioneers began to settle in outlying regions.

The Revolutionary War and treaties with the French, English, and the Indians did not, however, automatically end the land disputes in what would become Ohio and the Old Northwest Territory. Individual states, which often conflicted as much with each other as with the fledgling government established by the Articles of Confederation, claimed chunks of the West.

The few Indians who remained east of the Cuyahoga River in the nineteenth century were friendly with the settlers. According to local legend, the dormitories of Andrews Institute in Willoughby occupy the site of the last Lake County Indian village. This photo was taken by the Meinke-Eldred Flying Service, Willoughby, in the mid-twentieth century. Courtesy, Lake County Historical Society

(Far Left) Moses Cleaveland of Canterbury was one of the directors of the Connecticut Land Company as well as the company's general agent for conducting the surveying expeditions in the Western Reserve. In honor of his leadership, the town laid out on the banks of the Cuyahoga River was given his name. Years later, the spelling of the city's name was changed to "Cleveland." Courtesy, Western Reserve Historical Society

(Left) Astronomer Seth Pease accompanied both the 1796 and 1797 surveying expeditions into the Western Reserve and kept a journal that details the purchase of supplies, a meeting with representatives from the Six Nations of the Iroquois, and David Eldridge's drowning as he attempted to swim his horse across the Grand River. Courtesy, Western Reserve Historical Society

As were others, Connecticut's claim was based on a vague 1630 conveyance of title that read:

All that part of New England, in America, which lies and extends itself from a river there called Narragansett river, the space of forty leagues upon a straight line near the sea shore, towards the south-west, west by south, or west, as the coast lieth, towards Virginia, accounting three English miles whatsoever, lying and being within the bounds aforesaid, north and south in latitude and breadth, and in length and longitude, and within all the breadth aforesaid throughout all the main lands there, from the western ocean to the South Seas.

One by one the coastal states agreed to cede their western lands to the United States government. Connecticut, however, was adamant in its refusal to relinquish claims to western lands because of the tremendous losses it had sustained during the Revolution, and because of its thwarted attempts to settle the lands it had claimed in the Wyoming country of eastern Pennsylvania. Although Connecticut lost its claim to the Pennsylvania lands in 1782, it was allowed to reserve a similar amount of territory in northern Ohio when it finally gave up the remainder of its western lands in 1786. The area to which Connecticut retained claim was to be administered as a colony of the mother state and would be known as Connecticut's Western Reserve. Near its eastern edge lay the land that was to become Lake County.

After setting aside about 525,000 acres as "Sufferer's Lands" (also called Firelands), the State of Connecticut sold the remaining Western Reserve acreage to the newly organized Connecticut Land Company for $1.2 million (about 35 cents an acre).

The purchasers and their proprietors chose one of their own directors, Moses Cleaveland, to lead the initial expedition of 50 men and two women into the wilderness. Over the next few years surveyors traveled the Western Reserve during the warm months, mapping the area for later sale and making notes about their explorations. Eighteen-year-old John Milton Holley kept a journal of his experiences during the 1796 expedition and on October 20 described his journey past the Grand River and what would become Perry Township.

"The Western Reserve is situated in the northeast quarter of the state between Lake Erie on the north, Pennsylvania East. It extends 120 miles from East to West and upon an average 52 from north to south," reads the historic map of the Western Reserve published by William Sumner of Portage County in the early 1800s. Courtesy, Western Reserve Historical Society

About 36 miles from Cuyahoga Creek, is a burning spring in the lake, 2 or 3 rods from shore, which [is] very perceptible as you stand upon the beach, from its boiling motion. Mr. Porter told me that he, with General Cleaveland and Mr. Stow, had made a trial to know if it was inflammable, which they found to be the case, although it was [a] very unfavorable time when they did it. The waves ran high and the wind blew hard. They held a torch, well lighted, very close to the water, when there appeared a flame like that of spirits burning, but it was so much mixed with other air and the water so deep over four feet, that the flame would go out immediately.

According to Indian legend this spring was the home of the Big Water God which swarmed with fish that were regarded as a special gift of the god when he was in a good humor.

On the eve of westward migration, the Lake County frontier was a land shaped by legends, the forces of ancient ages, and the claims of many different peoples—some long forgotten. Pioneers from the North Atlantic states, Pennsylvania, and the Isle of Man who came to settle over the next 50 years would further impact the land and the future as their ideas fashioned the wilderness into the community known today as Lake County, Ohio.

In 1907 the construction of the current Lake County courthouse began on the square. Today the courthouse still serves as the hub for governmental activity. Courtesy, Lake County Historical Society

CREATION OF A COMMUNITY

In February 1800 Colonel Eleazar Paine joined General Edward
Paine in Aurora, New York, for a journey to the Western Reserve.
Fellow traveler Hendrick E. Paine, writing in 1877, recounted that

*. . . they started with sleighs, expecting to come up the lake on the ice. When
they got to Cattaraugas they found the ice unsafe. They built huts and left
the family there, to come on in boats when the lake opened. General Paine
and my father [Eleazar], with one or two others, came through with the
horses and commenced preparing for the family. The family at Cattaraugas
found themselves in the midst of a maple grove. They tapped the trees and
made a large quantity of maple sugar. When the lake opened they came
up in open boats.*

This map of Concord Township shows how old routes such as the Old Gridled Road, the Painesville-Warren Road, and the Painesville-Revenna Road traversed Lake County township. By 1875 over a dozen of the roads had been cut throughout the area. This map appears in the 1976 publication *Concord Township, Lake County, Ohio.* Courtesy, Lake County Historical Society

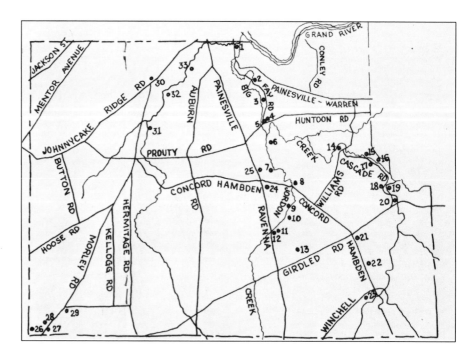

During the first decades of migration, two major trails led to the Western Reserve. Many New Englanders followed the Mohawk Valley across New York to the eastern tip of Lake Erie. From there they could brave the treachery of the lake by sailing along the coast to their destination or by following the Lake Trail, which led them along the natural sand ridges that had once marked the edge of the ancient lake. The alternative was to head south and then west across the Pennsylvania mountains, turn northwest at Pittsburgh, and then on to the trail that led pioneers through Youngstown and Warren.

The need for additional migration routes had been recognized early, and in 1798 the directors of the Connecticut Land Company set aside $2,600 for a road from the western Pennsylvania border to Cleveland. When it was completed, the Old Girdled Road, named for the practice of encircling tree trunks with cuts for easier felling, passed through several Ashtabula County communities, Thompson Township in Geauga County, and Leroy and Concord townships now in Lake County, then meandered westward into Cleveland along the current route of Euclid Avenue. A few years later the first road opened leading from the southern portion of the Reserve to Lake Erie. Known today as Old State Road, this was probably first called the State Road, or the Painesville-Warren Road, a name descriptive of the

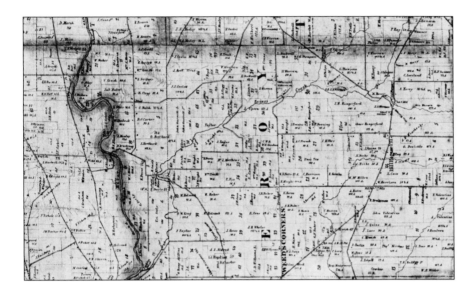

The Landowner's Map of 1857 is an important historical and genealogical research tool. This portion shows Leroy Township, which was one of the least populated areas in the 1840s and 1850s, despite its early settlement. Originally the Grand River did not form the county's entire northern boundary and the northeastern section near Seeley Road and Paine's Hollow belonged to Perry Township. Courtesy, Lake County Historical Society

northern and southern points of termination. Another road was laid out by Captain Edward Paine of Chardon. From its point of origin in Painesville, it wound south through Mentor, Kirtland Flats, Chester, Aurora, and Hudson to the Old Portage and then followed the Tuscarawas River to Chillicothe, from whence the road took its name.

But whether they sailed down a lake well known for storms, or trudged along one of the muddy trails, most of the early pioneers trudging through northern Geauga County in search of a new home shared a common New England heritage. Many emigrated directly from homes in coastal states such as Connecticut and Massachusetts, while those who came from western New York and northern Pennsylvania were often no more than a few generations removed from ancestral homes in New England. The few who did not share in this tradition often came from as far away as the Isle of Man.

What compelled these people to pack their worldly belongings along with their faith and their dreams into wagons or ships heading west into the wilderness? Difficult economic conditions and the scarcity of land were probably the primary reasons for moving westward. Perhaps some were driven by restlessness, particularly that which comes after the resolution of a major conflict such as the Revolutionary War or the War of 1812.

Unusual weather conditions also spurred emigration, especially during the summer of 1816 which was so cold and dry that many

After a successful trading venture in the Western Reserve in 1796 and 1797, Edward Paine bought 1,000 acres of land near the Grand River, organized a group of 66 settlers from among his New York neighbors, and journeyed to what became Lake County. A community builder, he laid out the Chillicothe Road, hosted the Reverend Joseph Badger during his travels, and gave his name to a township and a city. Courtesy, Lake County Historical Society

crops failed. What farmers did not know was that their famine was the result of an unusual and devastatingly dense cloud of particles hovering over the Northern Hemisphere. Such atmospheric interference from volcanic eruptions half a world away in Indonesia resulted in increased migration to the Western Reserve, an area perceived by some as a land of promise and future.

Whether the early pioneers truly believed the frontier to be such a paradise is questionable, but that did not stop them from writing of their new home in glowing terms. Perhaps the most persuasive arguments for migration came from family and friends. William Kelly wrote several letters home to relatives on the Isle of Man enthusiastically describing the availability of jobs, potential earning power, and the cheapness of provisions as well as the favorable social conditions. This may be the reason that many early settlements were dominated by members of the same family.

Public propaganda also encouraged emigration. A ballad written by Colonel Edward Paine and published in a newspaper in Hartford County, Connecticut, in 1803, proclaimed that:

Ye swaines who are virtuous, healthy, and wise, Who are possessed of activity and enterprise, Who from the truth and sobriety never will swerve, Come emigrate with me to the Western Reserve. Near the banks of proud Erie, my friends, we will go, To lands that with milk and with honey o'er flow; Near the mouth of Grand River you will clearly observe A beautiful country called "Western Reserve." At "Elysian Point" General Paine made his stand, And Walworth at "Blooming Grove," quite near at hand, For encouraging migration many thanks they deserve From every proprietor of the Western Reserve.

Although Paine's ballad was aimed toward a general promotion of the Western Reserve, his mention of several points of interest such as the Grand River, Elysian Point, and Blooming Grove hinted at his own preference for the land which would become Lake County.

Ironically, the first recorded tornado in the history of Ohio passed through Geauga County not long after Paine's ballad appeared. Perhaps it was an omen. Delightful as the Western Reserve might be, Paine's rosy picture could not disguise the grim reality of pioneering any more than it could disguise the harshness of the trails leading west.

As the roads opened, communities developed, particularly along the lake and river shores. Mentor Marsh, the first settlement, had been cleared and a crop of winter wheat planted by Charles Parker and his wife, Ebenezer Merry, and several others in the summer of 1797. By 1811 at least one family resided in each township of what would become Lake County.

Food and shelter were the primary concerns of pioneers. Most early settlers followed a pattern of settlement similar to that of Captain Truman Griswold, a celebrated hunter from Oswego County, New York, who in 1810 purchased land on the main road from Painesville to Willoughby. In typical pioneer style, the family built a log house, cleared timber, and fenced their land. With food and shelter somewhat assured, they repeated the cycle by purchasing additional land, building a more "customary domicil," then returning to the task of clearing timber. This account of Griswold's homestead from the reminiscences of E.J. Ferriss simplifies the sweat and toil that early families expended in their efforts to begin a new life on the Lake County frontier. Numerous difficulties had to be surmounted, including the tackling of the dense forests which posed considerable problems for the farmer eager to plant a corn patch and vegetable garden. Armed with little more than determination, a sharp ax, and a fagot, the pioneers attacked the giant trees until the deadenings created by girdling the trees and the log heap fires became a common sight.

According to Eleazar Paine's recollections, inclement weather also plagued the pioneers.

Christmas 1806 was exceedingly warm, and the weather continued moderate until January 12, 1807. It then began to snow and continued snowing until the 16th and snow fell between 12 and 14 inches deep, and the winter continued much colder than was ever known in the country before until the 24th; then thawed a few days; then continued much colder than before, so extremely cold that several people were found frozen to death. March 10th the snow all went off and it was very warm. The 18th . . . snow fell from 4 to 6 inches in depth. March 29th Grand River broke up after being shut 3 months. March 30 snowed, 31 fair; April 1st, snowed; April 2nd, snowed; which made the snow about 12 inches deep. April 25 Grand River rose so as to flood all the flats and carried off a considerble fence. 1807 continued extremely wet the whole season. Jan. 1st the river rose extremely high.

Snow was only a part of the problem. Christopher Crary later reminisced that the summer of 1816 was very cold and little corn ripened. That next spring several farmers journeyed to Tuscarawas County to buy corn while their families and livestock lived on the nutritious, but rather distasteful, wild onions that tainted the breath and lent the cow's milk a sickening smell and unpalatable flavor. But Lake County weather could be more than uncomfortable; it could be life-threatening. During the 1811 tornado, a tree fell on the Minor cabin, missing the children who had huddled under their sleepers but instantly killing their father.

Wild beasts threatened human life as well as livestock. Small parties of hunters pursued marauding panthers, wolves, and bears throughout the wilderness in efforts to obliterate them but were unable to prevent the deaths of some of the early settlers. Crary remembered that in Kirtland one 15-year-old boy disappeared in the woods. The next spring a lock of hair, some buttons, and bits of clothing were found and the neighbors concluded that he had been devoured by some wild beast.

The dangers of the wilderness were aggravated by an economy based on subsistence farming and "cabin industry," in which each family produced as much of its own goods as possible. This included not only food and flour but also candles, soap, clothing, shoes, tools, and furniture. Currency was scarce due to the lack of banks, and the early settlers relied on the barter system for goods that they could not manufacture themselves. Maple sugar, homemade peach brandy, and whiskey could be traded for goods or labor.

Despite the hardships, there were good times. In 1877 Hendrick E. Paine reminisced that:

It was not all hard work and short fare. We had our amusements, and one of our greatest pleasures was to go to Gen. Paine's and spend the evening. His latch string always hung out; everybody was welcome. The General would sit down by his wife . . . pat her on the shoulder and say: 'come mother, sing and let the young folks dance.' She would sit and card tow, or spin on the little wheel, and sing dancing tunes all the evening. We always went home happy from there.

As the scattered and rather randomly settled areas began to flourish, town building began. In 1803 Abraham Skinner and Eleazar Paine laid out the village of New Market. Two years later Skinner laid out another town, this one for Henry Champion. Located in an area already known as Oak Openings, the town bore Champion's name for a short time before it was renamed Painesville in tribute to General Edward Paine. About 1808 Skinner aided Samuel Huntington in planning the village of Grandon, so named for its location on the Grand River and eventually renamed Fairport in honor of its lake harbor.

Despite the varying rate of growth in the individual townships, migration did progress. As the population increased, the creation of counties and townships in the Western Reserve proceeded rather rapidly for purposes of more effective local government. In 1797 that portion of the Reserve lying to the east of the Cuyahoga River was included in a very large Jefferson County. In 1800 Jefferson County was redistributed into the new County of Trumbull which was created to include what is now known as the Western Reserve. Six years later Trumbull County was further divided into Geauga and Trumbull counties. Geauga comprised land which would someday be the counties of Ashtabula, eastern Cuyahoga, Lake, and Geauga, while the remaining portions retained the name of Trum-

The village of Grandon was laid out in 1812 by Abraham Skinner, Samuel Huntington, Seymour and Calvin Austin, and Simon Perkins to provide the area with a port, and was appropriately located on the east side of the Grand River along the Lake Erie shore. By 1836 the village was incorporated as Fairport. Courtesy, Lake County Historical Society

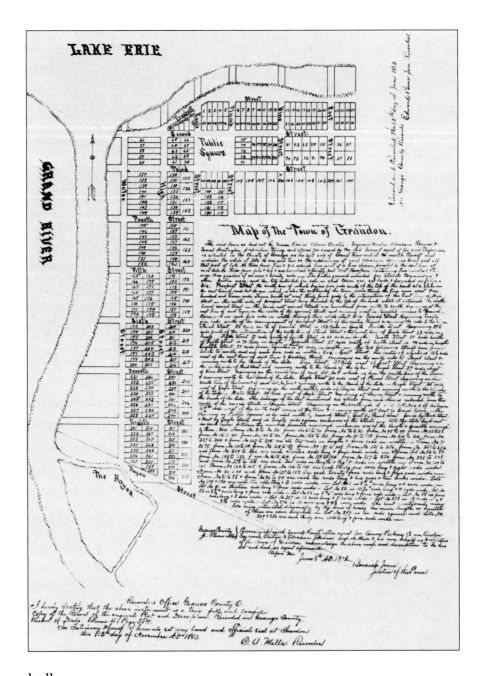

bull.

"I hope and believe the court house will be fixed on my square," Henry Champion wrote to Abraham Skinner in August of 1806. Champion echoed the sentiments of citizens throughout Geauga County who realized that the designation of their village as the principal seat of justice would assure both population and commercial growth. To Champion's disappointment, his town was overlooked in 1806 in favor of nearby New Market. Two years later the remainder of

the population of northern Geauga County (later to become Lake County) experienced a similar disappointment when the county seat was moved to Chardon, a more centrally located spot despite its lack of population.

Wealthy Bostonian Peter Chardon Brooks donated the land for the village plat to the County of Geauga (which then included most of current Lake County) on the condition that it be named "Chardon," the French word for "thistle." This was done, and the county seat became official in June of 1808. This arrangement lasted only one year before Henry Champion's arguments to locate the seat in his town were successful. By 1811, however, the seat was once again removed to Chardon which, to this day, remains the seat of Geauga County. By the time the Geauga County Court met in the new Chardon Courthouse in the fall of 1813, Geauga County had been further divided by the creation of Ashtabula County and Cuyahoga County, which then included Chagrin Township.

The first courthouse in Geauga County was built by Abraham Skinner of hewn black walnut logs and was located at New Market in Painesville Township. The court and commissioners met here until June of 1808 when the county seat was officially moved to Chardon. Courtesy, Lake County Historical Society

From 1811 to the 1840 creation of Lake County, the village of Chardon served as the seat of justice. This 1846 drawing by Henry Howe shows the east side of the square with the church and brick courthouse. Built over the 1820s, its overhanging roof was supported by eight columns two stories high. From *Historical Collections of Ohio,* 1861

Just as the boundaries and names of the early counties shifted and changed, so did those of the townships which would eventually form Lake County. By 1822 those which today comprise Lake County had assumed their current boundaries and names but the creation of Lake County itself was much longer in coming. The controversy over the location of the county seat continued through the next two decades. Viewing the geographical entirety of Geauga County, the location of the seat of justice on a Chardon Township hilltop seemed ideal. By 1820, however, the Painesville area had clearly become the population center, not only of the county, but also of the Western Reserve. When suggestions for moving the county seat to Painesville were adamantly opposed, leading citizens of the northernmost townships began to explore the possible division of Geauga into two counties.

A MEETING of the citizens of Painesville Township, in favor of the erection of a new County, will be held at the Town House in said Painesville, at 2 o'clock on Saturday the 2nd day of November next, for the purpose of conceting measures necessary to accomplish that object.

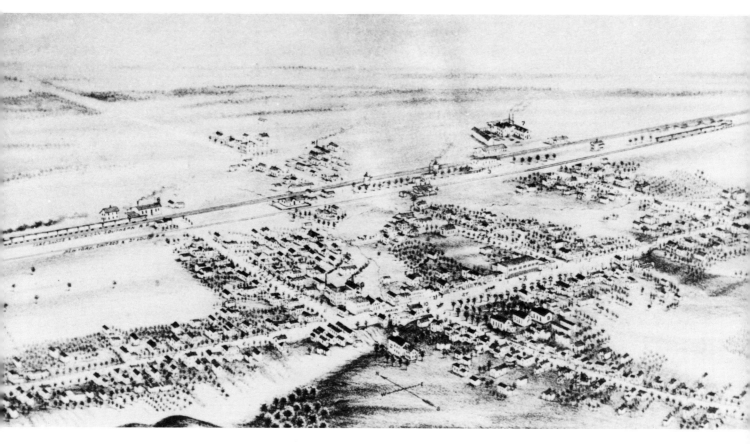

The names of 57 citizens immediately followed this announcement, published in the October 22, 1839, edition of the Painesville *Telegraph* and accompanied by a notice of application to the Ohio General Assembly for the erection of a new county to embrace the townships of Kirtland, Concord, LeRoy, north Thompson, Madison, Perry, Painesville, Mentor, Willoughby (then part of Cuyahoga County), and "that portion of the State of Ohio, lying north of the five last mentioned Townships," namely Lake Erie. The inclusion of the lake to the International Boundary was crucial in meeting state requirements for a minimum county acreage of 400 square miles by which the proposed Lake County fell short by 159 square miles.

Writing 100 years later, historian Frederick C. Waite reported that when Geaugans met in Chardon in December of 1839 to discuss the "Lake County" application, they passed a resolution in which "they said that they were just as anxious to have Painesville get out of Geauga County as Painesville was desirous of getting out

By 1808 families from Berkshire County, Massachusetts, and Willington, Connecticut, were building a community called Centreville in Chapin Township. Just a year before, the village had been a part of Richfield Township and in 1811 it would become a permanent part of Madison Township. By 1883 when this aerial view was taken, Centreville had been renamed Madison Village and boasted a population of almost 800. Courtesy, Lake County Historical Society

A farm residence such as this was only a pioneer's dream in the early 1800s. It took many years to clear the heavily forested Ohio hills for farming and, during that time, rude cabins usually sufficed for shelter. This farm belonged to Stephen H. Hart of Mentor, Ohio. From *Lake County Illustrated*, 1912. Courtesy, Lake County Historical Society

but that the Geauga people were unwilling that Painesville should take any other townships with it."

Today we can only guess at the arguments that raged between northern and southern Geaugans. Painesville was the population center of the county and, as such, deserved to be the county seat, northerners might have contended. Painesville was too far away from those in southern Geauga and Chardon was, in 1839, centrally located in the county, southerners might have responded.

Waite speculated that on the political front there was a factional fight within the popular Whig Party of Geauga County and some "bitter contests" between leading personalities in that party. Reports of legislative proceedings printed in the *Telegraph* suggest such conclusions. On January 21, 1840, the paper reported that "in the House, on the 13th Mr. Morse presented a petition from the citizens of Cuyahoga and Geauga Counties, for the new county of Lake. Mr. Ford [presented a petition] from citizens of Geauga, remonstrating against the same." On February 4, Editor L.L. Rice stated in print that there was no further news of the new county. "We notice in the proceedings of the legislature frequent mention of petitions presented by Messrs. Bissell and Morse, and remonstrated by Mr. Ford. They are referred, of course, to the appropriate committee."

One week later, Rice informed his subscribers that the bill had lost by a vote of 33 to 29 but "it is thought by some that it will be re-considered and pass the House." Items in the February 18 edition of the *Telegraph* hinted at the personal politics involved in Lake County's creation.

It is said that one leading object with some members in creating this new county is to destroy Mr. Ford's influence. He opposes the bill and the leaders have found it necessary to take some measures to destroy him. His influence has been too much for them; and it was thought a good opportunity as he is warmly opposed to this county, to turn in and make an effort to create it, and by appealing to party they will probably effect the passage of the bill, but not the destruction of Mr. Ford's influence, if that is their object.

If Rice's conjectures were false, he printed no arguments against them in his newspaper although he continued to report the progress of the bill as several amendments were suggested and rejected. One, however, was accepted: that "no tax shall be levied for erecting public buildings." With that stipulation the bill passed the Ohio House with a vote 38 to 30. Its passage by the Ohio Senate was considered certain, according to Rice, who in the March 3 edition suggested "the friends of the measure [have] every confidence of its success. Our next paper will probably be published in the county of Lake."

The matter was not quite so simple, however, and just days later a meeting was called to discuss ways to further promote the passage of the bill. But the difficulties must have been minor for on March 20, 1840, Lake County was established and the elections set for April 6. The *Telegraph* admonished "Whigs of Lake County—the manner in which you discharge your duty at the first County Election under

Begun in 1840, the construction of the first Lake County courthouse was not completed until 1852, although officials began using it several years earlier. Today this building still stands on the square and serves as Painesville City Hall. Courtesy, Lake County Historical Society

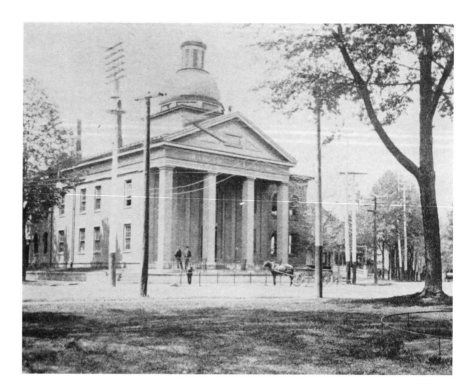

the same banner will affect the cause of Harrison and Reform." The presidential election of Whig candidate William Henry Harrison versus Democrat Martin Van Buren had never been far from the minds of area politicians and had usually appeared on the front page of the *Telegraph*, overshadowing the news of the creation of Lake County. The Whig victory in the Lake County elections seemed a positive omen for the upcoming presidential election and was linked to the national campaign by headlines boasting:

LAKE COUNTY ELECTION. SPLENDID WHIG VICTORY! 1000 MAJORITY! Every township for Harrison. FIRST COUNTY RALLY. The whole regular Whig Ticket elected by from 994 to 1004 Majority!!! The result is a most gratifying and glorious victory—unexpected in the strength of the Whigs, and glorious in its every aspect and bearing. The Whigs of Lake County have done themselves great credit, by their prompt rally, and their successful resistance of the attempts to divide and distract them.

On this tide of enthusiasm, citizens of the new county collected monies for the construction of a courthouse even before a formal committee was appointed. Completed in 1852, that building still stands today

on the western edge of the Painesville square, serving not as a courthouse, however, but as the Painesville City Hall.

Nearby, the current Lake County Courthouse, built in 1907, stands as a monument to the growth of Lake County's government which serves a population that has expanded from 13,719 people in 1840 to over 220,000 in 1988. And as that population grew, so did the expectations of those who chose to live in Lake County. Many of these expectations were directly related to the life the residents had known before their emigration. Primary among them was the need for opportunities to practice the religion of their choice, to educate their children, and to foster a sense of unity within their chosen community. Under the guidance of leaders who looked back to their roots as well as forward into the future, Lake County quickly passed from a frontier to a county of settled rural villages and townships marked with the distinctive stamp of the New

As the seat of Lake County, Painesville continued to grow, as this 1886 photo by George W. Barnard shows. Henry Howe included this in his second edition of the *Historical Collections of Ohio*, at a time when Painesville's population numbered approximately 4,200. By 1890 Lake County boasted a total population of 18,235. From *Historical Collections of Ohio*, 1888

Although public education was readily available by the late nineteenth century, some students chose to attend private schools, often in preparation for higher education. M.D. Mathews, daughter-in-law of Painesville physician John Mathews, operated a "Family School" which offered preparatory classes for students who hoped to attend Lake Erie Female Seminary from the 1870s until 1900. One of her classes is shown above, circa 1890s. Courtesy, Lake County Historical Society.

SHAPING OUR EVERYDAY LIVES

"If you have no good school near you, I shall leave my children perhaps at Pittsburgh," wrote Thomas Skinner to his brother Abraham in 1811. Thomas' words, penned in Pennsylvania, suggest that provisions, tools, family pictures, and assorted precious belongings were not the only cargo which settlers carted into the virgin territory. Equally important were their ideas about the family, the community, and the forces that would shape their everyday lives.

For Thomas, as for many of the New England tradition, these forces included a firm commitment to education.

Instruction in reading, writing, and arithmetic was often handled within the home until formal schools could be built, and teachers were supported by the community. Often, several families joined together in the effort and one of the adults would oversee the education of the children. In some communities, the school term encompassed only the three winter months, and might be as intensive as six or seven hours a day for six days a week. Curriculum was usually determined by the textbooks on hand and might include lessons from various readers, spelling books, and the Bible.

Much of a student's early educational experience was also shaped by the knowledge of the teacher who might have been chosen less for experience than for willingness to accept the position at its low rate of pay. Young men often sought such teaching jobs as a way to earn their college tuition and usually received about $10 per month plus board. Young women, however, usually commanded less than $4 per month plus board, despite their professional credentials. Under these conditions, turnover in the early teaching profession was rather high.

Despite the problems of education, most area townships had some type of grammar school by the 1820s. Later in that decade, the beginnings of Lake County's public school system were apparent when township trustees began to levy taxes for the building of schoolhouses under the Ohio Legislature's first common school law. Following improvements at the state level, a board of education was elected in Painesville in 1851. Board members arranged townwide tax support to consolidate the neighborhood schools, and reorganized the existing system to accommodate graded classes. The Paines-

The Painesville Academy was a private high school which opened in 1823. Years of constant financial struggle ended when it was incorporated in 1829 as the Painesville Education Society and the building shown here was erected on Washington Street. Courtesy, Lake County Historical Society.

ville Public Schools began officially in 1852 after taking over the Painesville Academy, which would serve as the high school. Other Lake County communities followed suit.

A high school education was an accomplishment indeed, but still not as high as a Lake County student could aspire even as early as the 1830s. Healthful, pastoral settings attracted seminaries and collegiate institutions, particularly at the west end of the county, although the Madison Seminary on Middle Ridge Road operated successfully for almost 40 years in eastern Lake County.

In Kirtland, the abundance of abandoned buildings, a result of the Mormon exodus in the late 1830s, aided in Nelson Slater's choice of a location for his teacher's seminary. The school opened in September of 1839 after Slater obtained a lease for the use of the deserted temple and a state charter for the Western Reserve Teacher's Seminary and Kirtland Institute. The institute was designed for students with no intention of teaching, while the seminary course of study focused on the training of teachers of both sexes with an emphasis on quality as the key to the improvement of public education. The school operated into the early 1850s, at

At the eastern end of Lake County, the Madison Seminary offered private high school education for 40 years. At its peak, it enrolled 150 students and its buildings included a boarding facility which housed about half of the student body. Courtesy, Lake County Historical Society

which time it went into a general decline, possibly because of financial problems and keener competition for students from the other schools in the county.

The community of Chagrin entered an exciting period of development when the Willoughby University of Lake Erie was established in the fall of 1834. Although the founders began by creating a medical college, they hoped that eventually the university would expand to include separate colleges for women, men, and theology. The medical college had been chosen as their first endeavor because the only other such Ohio institution was in Cincinnati. Financial difficulties plagued the school from the beginning but, more seriously, it lost much of its community support in the 1840s when its faculty was accused of complicity in grave robbing to obtain bodies for dissection and teaching purposes. The disputes, which sometimes resulted in mobs storming the school, continued for more than six years, during which time some of the faculty became affiliated with Western Reserve College, then in Hudson. This group organized the Cleve-

For almost 20 years the Western Reserve Teachers' Seminary and Kirtland Institute attempted to provide quality education for area students. Classes met in the deserted Mormon Temple for a year before moving to the Methodist Church for 10 years, and then moving into their own building. Courtesy, Lake County Historical Society

land Medical College, the forerunner of today's School of Medicine of Case Western Reserve University. In 1847 the remainder of the university's medical department transferred to Columbus, Ohio, under the name of the Willoughby Medical College. The Columbus institution was eventually renamed the Starling Medical College of the Ohio State University.

And so the first medical college in the Western Reserve faded into history, but not before the little community of Chagrin could rename itself "Willoughby" in honor of the university's benefactor, Dr. Westel Willoughby, who would himself become the object of local legend.

"Ever since I was in the fourth grade in our local schools, I have been hearing the old story of how Dr. Westel Willoughby succeeded in inducing the 'powers that were' at that time to change the name of our town from Chagrin to Willoughby," wrote Willoughby historian Frank N. Shankland in 1953. "According to the popular story, Dr. Willoughby promised to leave his entire property to the Willoughby Medical college after his death, if the name of the town were changed to Willoughby. The story further relates that after his passing, all the property that he left was a framed picture of himself which is now in Cleveland." Although this may well be true, Shankland revealed what he considered to be vindicating evidence gleaned from the memoirs of a medical college trustee.

When the Medical college started (upstairs in the Knieling Block, November 1834) the teachers were very much dissatisfied with their quarters and demanded that the trustees provide a new building. The trustees arose to the occasion and received contributions which Totaled $1215.00. Soon after, they received from Dr. Willoughby of Herkimer, New York a generous gift of $1200.00.

In addition to the money, Shankland suggested that the memoirs of Willoughby resident Francelia Worallo indicated that Dr. Willoughby had offerred his library to the fledgling college if the village were named after him, "a promise that he sacredly fulfilled."

No matter what the deal, the town was obviously satisfied with it for when Dr. Willoughby died in 1835, his portrait was accepted. In April of that year, the name "Willoughby" was painted on the post office and the university retained his name through the disintegration of the medical college and the creation of the female seminary in 1847.

The seminary was clearly modeled on Mount Holyoke Seminary of South Hadley, Massachusetts, which had been operating successfully for 10 years under the watchful eyes of founding principal Mary Lyon, who aided the Willoughby trustees by recommending several of the first faculty members. The new institution was so popular that the newly constructed boardinghouse could not accommodate the

On the back of this photo Henry Holcomb wrote that the Painesville Brass Band "played at the laying of the corner-stone exercise of Lake Erie Female Seminary, July 4, 1857. It also played at the Opening of the Cowles House Hotel the same year, at which time an ambrotype was taken by F. Clapsadel." A photo was made of the ambrotype by Wynne Smith in March 1908. Courtesy, Lake County Historical Society

influx of students, and leading families in the community found themselves accepting young ladies as boarders. Student enrollment increased until the bright promise of the seminary's future was shattered by a tragic fire which burned the school to the ground.

Although many citizens were in favor of rebuilding the seminary in Willoughby, questions arose concerning the location and the size of the village. Elyria was interested in relocating the seminary there but the bid was rejected because of that town's proximity to Oberlin College. In the end, the seminary trustees chose Painesville and renamed the institution Lake Erie Female Seminary. Once again the Mount Holyoke Plan served as the model and faculty administrators were chosen for the South Hadley institution. This time the school acquired permanence in the community. By 1898 it had achieved college status. Today we know it as Lake Erie College.

Lake Erie Female Seminary's emulation of a New England institution is only one example of the strength of the ties between Lake County residents and their ancestral homes on the East Coast. The pointed spires of Protestant churches gleaming white against

"True education" was the goal of Lake Erie Seminary and College during Principal Mary Evans' tenure from 1868 through 1909. Preparation for both careers and wifehood included health, hygiene, and a broad collegiate education. This biology class was held during the 1898-1899 school year in the new Bentley Hall of Science where "the laboratories are well furnished for scientific work," according to the 1898 Viewbook. Courtesy, Lake County College Archives

the emerald lawns of village squares throughout the county remain a visual record of religious development that began in the early 1800s.

Because isolated frontier settlements rarely had enough population to support their own minister, religious instruction was provided by family members between the infrequent visits of circuit-riding preachers who spent their days riding from one settlement to another spreading the gospel of their church.

The Connecticut Missionary Society, a cooperative effort by the Congregational and Presbyterian churches, was organized in 1801 and its efforts dominated the religious scene for almost 25 years. The Reverend Nathan Darrow of the society led the effort to found Lake County's first church in 1810, aptly named the First Church. Darrow was able to conduct services only once a month because of the large amount of territory for which he was responsible, but the congregation grew nonetheless. By 1829 the membership had grown enough to warrant construction of a building for worship. The First Church was originally maintained by both the Congregational and Presbyterian churches until the dissolution of their union. At this time the First

Church became Presbyterian until 1862, when it switched to its current status as the First Church Congregational of Painesville. Other communities followed Painesville's example, and over the next 20 years ministers of the Connecticut Missionary Society aided in the organization of congregations at Kirtland and Chagrin.

Although the Congregationalists and Presbyterians were dominant in Lake County's religious life, ministers from other denominations were also active in the missionary effort. The Reverend Ira Eddy aided in establishing Methodist churches in Chagrin, Concord, Kirtland, Mentor, Painesville, and Wickliffe from 1815 to 1821. Although the Baptist Mission Society did not enter into the frontier missionary efforts until later in the century, Baptist congregations may have met informally as early as 1816 in Madison, Mentor, and Perry. Churches were organized in Leroy in 1826, in Perry in 1836, and reorganized in Madison in 1831. An Episcopal parish was organized in Painesville in 1824 and 10 years later its first church was erected on the site of the present St. James Church.

Although Protestant sects dominated Lake County in the nineteenth century, new religions grew in the fertile soil of the settled rural area. Pastor Sidney Rigdon of the Mentor Baptist Church was an early convert to the Church of the Disciples of Christ, whose followers preached a simple message based solely on the Bible, in revolt against the Presbyterian emphasis on creed and formal learning. Although congregations in Mentor, Painesville, and Willoughby accepted this new faith, which was often called Campbellism in deference to its founder, it was Rigdon's flock in Kirtland which followed him through his Campbellite teachings and into a communistic society which other congregations and even the Campbellite leaders would not accept. Within a year after this departure Rigdon and

(Above) Like many leading citizens, Willoughby lawyer Lord Sterling was involved in a variety of community activities. He helped found the First Presbyterian Church in 1835 as well as the female seminary in 1847, for which he hosted several young ladies in his home when the school's enrollment surpassed the accommodations. He also chaired the committee for village incorporation in 1853. He is shown here circa 1880. Courtesy, Lake County Historical Society

(Left) Reverend Ira Eddy's sermons to the pioneers were reputed to be colorful and enthusiastic despite the hardships he endured in spreading the gospel. Like many circuit riders, he preached at least once a day, often after a 10-mile ride over crude roads and through inclement weather. Courtesy, Lake County Historical Society and Painesville Methodist Church

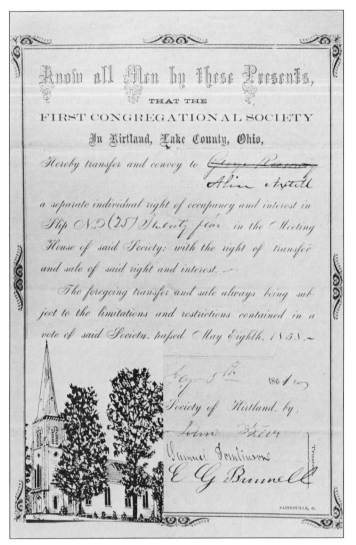

Paying for pews was a New England tradition in the early Western Reserve. This receipt was issued from the First Congregational Society in Kirtland. After meeting informally for a year, the members organized a church in 1819. In 1860 they formalized the name by which they had been called: The Old South Congregational Church. Courtesy, Lake County Historical Society

about 100 of his flock had accepted Mormonism. In February of 1831 Joseph Smith, Jr., and about 50 followers arrived at the Newell K. Whitney store in Kirtland and the Church of Jesus Christ of the Latter Day Saints began in earnest a decade of participation in the shaping of everyday lives in Lake County.

The pioneers' commitment to traditional education and religion provided a shaping force in the creation of communities from the wilderness, yet it was to the local newspapers that they looked for a unifying civic spirit.

At first settlers took advantage of Warren and Cleveland publications, but by 1822 they had their own newspaper through the efforts of Eber D. Howe. A native New Yorker, Howe had worked on papers in Buffalo and Erie before he moved to Cleveland in 1819 and began publishing the Cleveland *Herald*. Three years later he established the Painesville *Telegraph*, actively guiding its publication until 1835, when his brother Asahel assumed control. Despite changes in management and ownership, the *Telegraph* continued to serve the community until 1985 when the paper was put to bed for the last time. At the time of its dissolution the *Telegraph* was the oldest surviving newspaper in the Western Reserve as well as the first to be edited and published within Geauga and Lake counties. However, it was not the only newspaper in the area. Smaller community publications such as the Painesville *Republican,* the Willoughby *Republican,* the Willoughby *Independent,* and the Madison *Index* or also contributed to the communications network. And today, even though the *Telegraph* no longer appears on the doorstep daily, the *News-Herald,* based in Willoughby, continues the journalistic efforts begun so long ago for the purpose of keeping the public informed.

Smaller community publications have also contributed to the

communications network throughout the county's history. Some reflected the interests of opposing political parties while others concentrated on the villages and townships in which they were based. In the example of Fairport, the *Merchant News* and the *Fairport Beacon* were printed within the village by the Neal Printing Company between 1929 and 1959. These papers reported local news which reflected the diverse ethnic heritage that marked Fairport as unique in twentieth-century Lake County.

Although Fairport's earliest churches were traditionally Protestant, the immigrations of the Finnish, Hungarian, and Slovak peoples in the village at the turn of the century quickly distinguished

the village from its neighbors through the founding of the First Evangelical Lutheran Church, Soumi Zion Lutheran Church, Immanuel Evangelical Lutheran Church, Hungarian Reformed Church, and St. Michael's Byzantine Catholic Church. From such enrichment by Eastern European immigrants and the Catholicism brought by earlier Irish and German peoples, the village of Fairport reflects just a portion of the religious diversity found throughout the county in the 1980s.

(Above) Newspaperman Eber D. Howe influenced communications in Lake County when he founded the Painesville *Telegraph* in 1822. In his editorials he publicly supported various railroad ventures, Whig politics and the anti-slavery movement. With equal enthusiasm he slammed Mormonism, publishing his own work *Mormonism Unvailed* in 1834. Courtesy, Lake County Historical Society

(Above Right) Small community-based papers such as the *Madison Index* were often published weekly and provided news geared to a more specific local population. Items in this issue related that it had been a "slow week in Probate Court," only two couples had applied for marriage licenses, and that pantaloons would be worn "longer next month than they are this--about three days longer." Courtesy, Lake County Historical Society

Similar diversity may be found in today's educational opportunities. Western Lake County continues to be a forerunner in education, boasting such institutions as Lakeland Community College, Willoughby School of Fine Arts, and Andrews School for Girls. Andrews School was inspired by Willoughby College, a successor to both the Willoughby Collegiate Institute and the Willoughby Female Seminary. Margaret St. John had attended the college and, with her husband Wallace C. Andrews, founded Andrews School to provide a vocational secondary education for girls at nominal cost. Opened in 1910 in the former home of Dr. O.S. St. John at the corner of Erie and Vine streets, the school moved to its present campus in 1923 and today shares the grounds with the Willoughby School of Fine Arts, built in 1972. Operated by the Fine Arts Association, the school offers a student enrollment ranging in age from preschoolers through retirees in classes in visual arts, dance, theater, and music. Exhibitions, plays, operas, lectures, concerts, and a host of other visual and performing arts programs are presented for the Lake County public.

Nearby, Lakeland Community College offers fine arts programs within a curriculum designed to offer a liberal arts education as well

Churches published newspapers and newsletters to keep their congregations informed. These usually appeared monthly and included inspirational pieces as well as items about church activities. Courtesy, Lake County Historical Society

as occupational preparation. The youngest institution for high learning in the county, Lakeland was voted into existence by Lake Countians in 1965 and granted a charter by the Ohio Board of Regents one year later. Five months after voters approved the trustees request for a $1.6-million operating levy, the first 1,100 students gathered in temporary quarters along the Grand River in Painesville for fall classes in September 1967. Throughout the 1970s the college completed work on its campus, located on a portion of the former Mooreland Estate in Mentor. Student enrollment rose to nearly 20,000 in the 1984-1985 school year. The campus has expanded to include such facilities as an engineering technology laboratory.

Today, over 20 years later, Lakeland Community College has become an integral part of the Lake County community, a successor in the old tradition of quality education that the pioneers unpacked at the end of the long journey to their new home.

The Little Mountain Club stage carried passengers from the nearby train station, up the steep grade to the private club at the west end of the crest. Randall Wade initiated the association of wealthy Clevelanders, who, as the Little Mountain Club, purchased the Stocking House in 1872 and remodeled it into their private retreat. Courtesy, Western Reserve Historical Society

BUSINESS AND PLEASURE

Despite inclement weather, marauding animals, and hard work, the settlers persevered, writing enthusiastically about their land and its agricultural potential. In 1821 Hendrick Paine of Leroy wrote, "The manners and customs of our Country are similar to yours, and to boast of the fertility of our soil and the spontaneous as well as cultivated production it affords, would only be travelling over the same ground which many others have gone before me."

As the primary need for food and shelter was satisfied, Lake County farmers shifted their energies from subsistence farming to

Abundant groves of maple trees provided a tasty treat for the pioneers who brought their tradition of sugar- and syrup-making with them from New England. For some the equipment has changed over the years, but the basic methods of tapping the trees and boiling the sap are relatively the same and sugar camps throughout the county provide spring sugaring activities for Lake Countians. Courtesy, Lake County Historical Society

the specialized agriculture that was best suited to the land. Dairy farming and the production of butter, milk, and cheese peaked during the mid-nineteenth century and remained an important part of the economy into the twentieth. Fruits thrived in the fertile soil as Turhand Kirtland noted in 1798, writing of the "fine, large strawberries" he had found upon his arrival at the Grand River. Apple orchards may already have been producing for, according to folklore, the old grove on Burton Street in Fairport was originally planted by Johnny Appleseed. Fruit farms and nurseries appeared next to pastures dotted with dairy cows as the cultivation of peaches, plums, grapes, berries, landscape greenery, and flowers proved profitable.

The physical isolation of farm life was bridged as families banded together in agricultural societies, the Grange, Farm Bureau, and 4-H for educational, recreational, and business purposes. In 1889 "Kate," a diarist from the Kewish-Clague family, recorded the details of a Lake County Farmer's Institute. Having a woman (Mary Kewish) on the committee was a novelty in itself, Kate surmised, "but when that woman boldly asked for one day, that novelty became a wonder." Kewish and her friends got their wish when the day was designated Woman's Day and "it seemed as if every woman had come and brought her neighbors. The courthouse was jammed, both in courtroom, jury rooms, hall and stairs and hundreds went away who could

Some say the best red woolens in the county came from Dodd's Mills in Pleasant Valley. Dodd and William Webster purchased the mill in 1855 and, when Webster retired, Thomas Dodd joined his father in the business. By 1874 the Willoughby Business Directory listed J.A. Dodd and Son as a "Manufacturer of Woolen Goods, Cloths, Cashmeres, Sheetings, Flannels, Tweeds, Stocking Yarns." Courtesy, Lake County Historical Society

not get in." Frances J. Casement chaired a program which reflected the concerns of farmers' wives, including topics such as Woman of the Farm, Pin Money, Rag Carpets, Temperance, Education for Farmers' Daughters, and Woman Suffrage. One of the highlights of the day was the address of Principal Mary Evans of Lake Erie Seminary who spoke on "Handwork and Headwork."

In another of Kate's journal entries, she suggested that farmers' wives should

Strike . . . I mean against the column of advertisements in the Household page of The Farmer. *It is a sin and a shame that we can't have one whole page all to ourselves when our husbands and brothers have so many. Of course, this is a practical paper and they are practical farmers but are we not practical farmers wives, I'd like to know? Just let them do the washing and ironing, the baking, boiling, canning, stewing and frying, the sewing, knitting, patching and darning that we do . . . and they will find there is something intensely practical about us.*

But for most Lake Countians, the days of self-contained family production waned considerably as mills for grinding wheat into

This chest, featuring turned legs and porcelain knobs, was made at Phelps Mill on Thompson-Leroy Road in Leroy Township. Early industry in Lake County included saw and grist mills powered by rushing streams and waterfalls, although a few establishments used animals or the wind to turn the wheels. Courtesy, Lake County Historical Society

flour, turning logs into boards, and carding wool sprang up along the rivers and streams of the county. Tanneries, smithies, furniture factories, and wagon works dotted the landscape, and general stores, post offices, and banks joined the churches and schools clustered around village parks and country crossroads. Commercial businesses boomed, as did industrial growth within the county.

Local deposits of bog iron discovered along the ridge in Madison, Perry, Leroy, Concord, and Mentor encouraged the early growth of industry in the form of forges and furnaces. Although local ore contained only 25 percent pure iron, it was suitable for foundry work and economical at six cents a pound, costing three times less than prime ore from outside the Reserve. In the 1900s mining would again become an important part of the county's economy. The twentieth-century objective, however, would no longer be iron ore, but rather the salt that lay more than 2,000 feet below the Lake Erie basin.

Between Lake County's iron ore and salt booms, some sought their fortunes in the California Gold Rush of 1849, with the intentions of investing their hard-earned money back home. Each of the 16 subscribers of the "Painesville, Ohio, Mining Association of Lake County" contributed $200 to an expense fund for the trip west. Dr. Samuel Mathew's letters to the Painesville *Telegraph* recount adventures as the group followed the well-worn prairie and mountain trails to California's Yuba River. "Those were discouraging times," Mathews wrote of their battle with mountain fever, the loss of their prospecting rocker in a flood, and their brush with wolves that wan-

From its inception in the 1850s, the Lake County Fair encouraged the exchange of new ideas in agriculture and friendly competition between farmers. Today the annual mid-September festival still celebrates the county's rural past and present as residents gather for agricultural and industrial exhibits, horse races, and a carnival-style midway. Courtesy, Lake County Historical Society

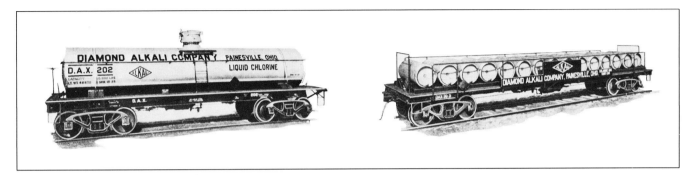

dered into their camp, put their paws up on the crude dinner table, and licked their plates. "We couldn't act as a company. We went by contract, divided, etc., had to separate."

"Am doing quite well," Mathews later assured his wife Huldah in 1850, writing from Nevada County. "I dislike abandoning mining and intended to do it only temporarily to accommodate Fobes. I got involved in his business and could not leave it to go up the river, got sick, and finally purchased his half mainly to make myself secure. So you see how I have got into this business *trading*, keeping public house, etc. I practice [medicine] a little, but not for the profits." Over a year later he expressed his reluctance to come home just yet, although he had been gone for over two years.

I have to consult circumstances, as I do not expect to have again such a chance for doing well in life, I mean so far as property is concerned, but the satisfaction of having done tolerably well, considering everything, and having had good health is not sufficient to reconcile me to remaining here any great length of time.

A few months later, Mathews sold the Eureka House, a boardinghouse of a "Superior Kind," according to the advertisement, and returned home.

If Huldah wondered at her husband's motives for training as a physician, then joining the Forty-niners only to end up trading goods and running a boardinghouse, she never questioned him in the letters that survive today. She may have suggested, however, that he could have run a mercantile establishment in his own backyard. The general stores that were established later in the nine-

In 1929 the Diamond Alkali Company added the production of liquid chlorine to an operation that already included basic sodium alkalies such as soda ash and bicarbonate of soda. Diamond played an important role in Lake County's economy for its establishment in Fairport in 1911 until it relocated to Texas in the 1980s. Courtesy, *Diamond Alkali Handbook,* second edition, 1929

Despite a name change to Randell Tavern from 1922 to 1932, the Rider Tavern is still one of the oldest taverns still in use west of the Alleghenies. When it first opened in 1810, it was a log hostelry, but it has been remodeled several times since. In the 1820s, master builder Jonathan Goldsmith added the porch columns. During the 1922 remodeling, the tavern was furnished in early American decor. Courtesy, Lake County Historical Society

teenth century were no less diversified than Abraham Skinner's warehouse at Skinner's Landing on the Grand River. Skinner's 1822 ledger lists the variety of goods he sold: chicken, apples, vinegar, cider, potatoes, beef, tea, corn, whisky, wheat, flour, leather for shoes, pork, plug tobacco, peach brandy, loads of wood, and bottled bitters.

Good inns, hotels, and taverns were also in demand, as footpaths and trails for ox carts gave way to macadam and plank roads for passenger stagecoaches. Only a few of these establishments survive today, including the Rider and Unionville taverns, but at one time numbers of them flourished. Over the nineteenth century 11 operated in downtown Willoughby. Fairport also boasted a variety, although today we might categorize them more as saloons than hotels. The most famous of these was Jones' Hall, ornately furnished with huge mirrors and a gilded bar.

The fortunes of the Fairport establishments were closely tied to lake commerce. The citizenry had early recognized the dangers of navigation on a lake with so few ports and adequate landings. Recognizing the potential of their own harbor, Fairporters sought to correct this with measures that William Darby noted in 1819. "The harbor is excellent for such vessels whose whole draft of water will admit entrance . . . Preparations are making to form wharves, extending

(Above) At the turn of the century, horse-drawn carriages braved the steep incline leading to the resort hotels at the crest of Little Mountain. Today, the horse and carriage shows at Lake Erie College's Morley Farm, on the North slope of the Little Mountain, recall the graciousness of this part of Lake County's past. Courtesy, Lake Erie College & Public Relations

(Right) Once a country estate, Morley Farm on the northern slope of Little Mountain is the site of the Lake Erie College Equestrian Center. The Manor House, originally the home of the Morley Family, is now the residence of the president of Lake Erie College. Courtesy, Lake Erie College Public Relations

(Above) In the 1980s, the football fields next to the Lakeland Community College Athletic and Fitness Center come alive with visitors as the college hosts the Cleveland Browns Training Camp from late July through August. Practices, free and open to the public, are well attended by Lake Countians. Courtesy, Lakeland Community College

(Right) Cleveland Browns quarterback Paul Mc Donald takes a break to sign autographs for fans during summer training at Lakeland Community College in the early 1980s. From late July through August, the football fields next to the Lakeland Community College Athletic and Fitness Center come alive as fans attend practices between classes. Courtesy, Lakeland Community College

YACHT RACING
MENTOR-ON-THE-LAKE, OHIO

White sails still dot Lake Erie as Lake Countians take to the water each summer to enjoy their favorite sports. In the 1940s, when this postcard appeared, the sails were frequently those of yacht racers. In the 1980s, the multicolored sails of the windsurfers dominate the view from Mentor Headlands Beach. Courtesy, Western Reserve Historical Society

Lakeland Community College offers performing arts opportunities for students through the Lakeland Singers and the Jazz Ensemble as well as classes in theater and music. Similar opportunities are extended to the community through Lakeland's Civic Chorus, Civic Dance Company, Civic Band, and Civic Orchestra. Visual arts opportunities are also available through artist receptions and student exhibitions. Courtesy, Lakeland Community College

Just east of Willoughby, a treelined lane leads to the main buildings of the Andrews School for Girls. Originally created by Mr. and Mrs. Wallace Andrews to provide vocational secondary education, the school began in what had once been the Willoughby residence of Dr. O.S. St. John before moving to the campus it presently shares with the Willoughby School of Fine Arts. Courtesy, Susan M. Post

Painesville Park of 1908 was a village green in the New England tradition, its shaded walks serving as a
quiet backdrop for the daily activities of county government and community celebration. In 1868 Chinese lanterns and banners
transformed the park into a fairy-
land of red, white, and blue for
Ulysses S. Grant's election to the
United States presidency. Courtesy, Western Reserve Historical
Society

(Above) The iron ore industry in Fairport spanned over 60 years from its beginning in 1879. In 1890 a Painesville *Telegraph* article described the flourishing dock activity as ore-carrying vessels were unloaded with Brown cantilever machinery, also called tramways, which were built on the same architectural principal as the cantilever bridge at Niagara Falls. Courtesy, Western Reserve Historical Society

(Left) This 1910 postcard depicts "the machine in the garden" as the train, a popular symbol of progress and industry, passes over an idealized Grand River. The stone bridge in the foreground was originally built in the 1850s for the first steam railroad in the county, the Cleveland, Painesville and Ashtabula. Courtesy, Western Reserve Historical Society

(Above) The winding trails of Holden Arboretum offer the best of Lake County's flaming autumn foliage. From Thayer Center (shown here) and the Corning Building (not yet built in this photo) nature enthusiasts can meander through forests of pine and maple around Buttonbush Bog, and past Pierson's Creek as it flows through the ravine. Courtesy, Holden Arboretum

(Right) The unspoiled settings of Lake County's parks, preserves, and country fields provide breathtaking vistas, especially when Canadian geese swing across the sky. Flocks crowd the ponds of Holden Arboretum and Lake Metroparks almost year-round, vying for the cracked corn tossed by park staff and amused observers. Courtesy, Lake Metroparks

beyond the bar in such manner as to afford a harbor to vessels of any draft."

Fairporters also lobbied to make Grand River a port of entry and sought the help of the Honorable B. Ruggles, who in 1820 wrote to Abraham Skinner from Washington, D.C., saying, "I always feel a cheerfulness in promoting the interests of any portion of the inhabitants of our State." Over the next decade, several appropriations by Congress provided for the erection of permanent docks and piers and an 1825 proposal for the construction of a brick lighthouse by noted architect Jonathan Goldsmith. The stone building which tops the hill today rises from the same spot as the Goldsmith structure, and operated from 1872 until 1925 when the "light that shone for one hundred years" was replaced by a combination light and foghorn station on the west breakwater pierhead. From the top of the hill, the lighthouse silently witnessed the changing fortunes of Fairport as the village, and the county, struggled for economic prosperity and stability.

From the 1826 launching of the schooner *United States,* Lake County's shipbuilding and forwarding trade centered at Fairport. But the lack of convenient and dependable transportation for the inland farms to the docks exacted its toll on lake commerce and

(Right) The barkentine *City of Painesville* was launched into Lake Erie from its construction site in Fairport in 1869. Shipbuilding began in Fairport in 1826 and by 1900 about 40 schooners, steamers, brigs, scows, and tugs had been launched. Courtesy, Fairport Harbor Historical Society

(Below) Flanked by employees, Frederick Wilkes and H.H. Coe posed outside the Coe-Wilkes Company at Jackson and St. Clair streets in Painesville for this early 1890s photo. For over half a century, the company produced steam engines and sawmill machinery, then the narrow tapers for the artificial gas lamps that lit the streets at night. Courtesy, Lake County Historical Society

on the farmers who struggled to get their crops to market.

In the 1830s Lake Countians courted the state legislature in hopes that the proposed Ohio Canal would connect with the Grand River. The loss of this canal to Cleveland was still being lamented in 1888 when George E. Paine wrote to the editor of the Painesville *Telegraph* urging the citizens of Painesville to forestall the ship canal project proposed for Cleveland in hopes that the Grand River could once again

be considered. To fill the void in the 1830s, plank and macadam roads were built to conquer the mud and provide more dependable access to the markets in Painesville and the Lake Erie docks. Over the next few decades, old bridges that could no longer contain the traffic were replaced. In May of 1866 the firm of McNair, Claflen and Company proposed to "construct a Highway Bridge in Home's [Patent Truss Bridge] most improved Plan across Grand River at Painesville, furnishing all materials, labor and Patent, etc. and according to plan herewith submitted for the Sum of: $25.50."

The railroads offered hope for boosting prosperity in the county, and as early as 1837 the Painesville and Fairport Railroad opened for business. Unfortunately the financial panic of 1837 and high water quickly ended the venture. Although several other attempts failed, persistence eventually paid off and in 1851 the iron rails of the Cleveland, Painesville and Ashtabula Railroad reached Painesville amidst a flurry of activity and celebration.

Similar excitement was generated in 1896 when the electric railway boom reached Lake County and interurban service between Willoughby and Cleveland opened with free rides for all. When the service reached Painesville a month later, the first electric car, with Miss Wright of Cleveland at the wheel, was greeted by a great crowd on foot, bicycles, and wagons as it rounded the curve onto State Street. Such success was followed by the opening of the Shoreline in 1898, the Fairport Line in 1901, and another quarter-century of service.

Headquartered in Willoughby, the Cleveland, Painesville, and Eastern Railroad, or the CP&E, as the interurban was usually called,

In 1946 the official souvenir program for Fairport's 50th anniversary presented the little village as "The Best Location in the Nation." The sentiment was indicative of the booster spirit sweeping the entire county. Picture from the *Official Souvenir Program*

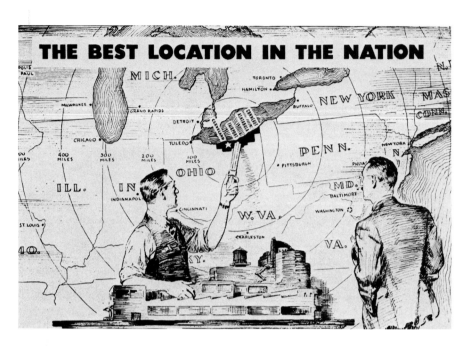

provided much-needed local transportation between the three northeastern Ohio counties on the lake. One observer wrote that "it was common to see passengers crowded on the rear platform steps of the popular late evening train from Cleveland." Motion sickness was also common as the cars swayed back and forth over the tracks. But the disadvantages were outweighed by the advantages, and at the turn of the century frugal Lake County residents could easily shop in Cleveland stores and sell their farm produce in urban markets.

The advent of modern transportation networks also broadened the recreational opportunities of Lake Countians who enjoyed such Cleveland amenities as Severance Hall operatic performances, while Clevelanders took advantage of the countryside. On an October Sunday in 1940 Willoughby diarist Sadie Talbot Eddy wrote: "A perfect Fall day… Dinner and work, then all went for a drive to see beautiful colored leaves." One wonders if on any of their jaunts, Sadie and her family passed Maria and John Wallace, Clevelanders charmed by Lake County. Maria later wrote:

In October, on one of our jaunts to see the fall coloring, I steered John onto the trail [where she hoped to convince him to build their summer home]. As he drove along the river, with the gorgeous reds and yellows of the leaves reflected in the clear water, with the sheer cliff rising in the background, where hundreds

of hemlocks blended with maples, beeches and oaks, he could not hide his
surprise.

Maria's summers in the 1930s and 1940s were not unlike those of
E.J. Ferriss who in his boyhood 100 years earlier spent "many a pleasant hour and jolly time . . . in company with the neighbors' boys
in rambling through the forest in search of sheepberries." Less innocent pursuits of Ferriss and his friends included raiding farmers'
cornfields to gather roasting corn for impromptu parties.

Little Mountain attracted picnickers who arose early in the morning to prepare for the ride along Johnnycake Ridge to Anderson's
Corners, then southwest for three or four miles through an uncultivated forest. Ferriss later recalled that "The road, if it might be
called a road," was cluttered by underbrush, girdled timber, and old
fallen trees "so that an expert driver might possibly get through with
only an occasional hitching of his craft on a snag." Less than a
mile from their destination, the party set out on foot "over logs,
through brush and brambles to the base of the cliff." From there
they climbed the rugged ascent to "promenade the eminences, examine the rocks, explore the caverns and, finding a smooth flat
rock, nicely carpeted with moss, near the southwest corner of the
bluff directly over a spring of pure, cool water, decided to spread
their viands on it."

Similar pursuits were carried out by patrons of the hotels that
sprang up on the crest of Little Mountain. The popularity of these
establishments boomed for both day trips and summer-long retreats. Numerous articles appeared in the *Telegraph* promoting such
recreation. On June 13, 1872, the editor suggested that "Just at this
time a drive from Painesville to Little Mountain is a most pleasant
and enjoyable one. The roads are in excellent condition, the natural
scenery is very fine and the handsome farms with their green fields
and nice residences, all combine to make the trip one not easily
surpassed." Two weeks later, the *Telegraph* announced that "Those
who are looking for a comfortable place, may find it at Little Mountain. A large number of guests are already enjoying its cool shades
and invigorating air and more are coming."

High jinks amused Little Mountain vacationers as they relaxed in the vigorating summer air for which the resort was famous. Photos taken from the nineteenth-century stereopticon views of H.L. Eggleston attest to the popularity of the area. Courtesy, Lake County Historical Society

Little Mountain was not the only recreational choice for vacationers in Lake County. As it does today, Lake Erie provided opportunities for enjoying fresh air, swimming, boating, and fishing. Travelers heading east along the shoreline might enjoy the attractions of Salida Beach at Mentor-on-the-Lake, Mentor Headlands, the Shore Club, or Linden Beach near Fairport. Willoughbeach Park, operating during the first decades of the twentieth century, offered elaborate accommodations for swimming, picnicking, and dancing, including a merry-go-round and popcorn and ice cream stands.

During the summers of the Progressive Era, Lake County also came alive as tourists and townspeople gathered on the village greens to hear the musical strains of local bands who performed on white-frame bandstands reminiscent of New England. But even as the need for public recreational areas grew, more and more of the land best suited to such ventures were bought by private owners.

Recognition of the need for private ventures to preserve Lake County's natural heritage accompanied the early twentieth-century park development of townships and municipalities. Today Holden Arboretum in Kirtland is one of the world's largest and most prestigious displays of trees and plant material. Its beginnings trace back to the 1913 death of Albert Fairchild Holden, who had established a trust for an arboretum to serve as a memorial to a daughter who had died young. After his death, his sister, Mrs. Benjamin Boles, pursued the project until the Kirtland Township site was confirmed and arrangements were made for the Cleveland Museum of Natural History to administer the preserve. The Boles family donated the first 100 acres in 1931, which began a pattern of expansion through donations of land and special funds. Today, the arboretum contains 2,800 acres of natural woodlands, horticultural collections, display gardens, ponds, fields, and ravines.

In 1958 development began of the Lake Metroparks. Although the county boasted less than 150,000 residents and over 75 percent of

Although resorts no longer line Lake Erie's shore, Lake Countians still take advantage of facilities such as the Mentor Harbor Yacht Club with its lagooned marina. Grand River and Fairport, shown in the extreme upper left, also provide recreation in the heat of the summer. Courtesy, Willoughby Historical Society

its land was still undeveloped, many community leaders recognized that the increasing rate of growth called for timely preservation measures if Lake Countians were to continue to enjoy their unique natural heritage. From the first parcel, which is known today as Helen Hazen Wyman Park on Big Creek in Painesville, Metroparks expanded its land base to 4,000 acres scattered throughout the county, preserving a diverse natural heritage. Today Lakeshore Parks offer access to Erie's unique shoreline while Gildersleeve Knob, one of the highest points in the county, towers above the surrounding Chapin Forest. Paine Creek in Paine Hollow takes its name from the family that settled near the falls which once generated power for saw and grist mills, while Penitentiary Glen, once part of the Samuel Halle farm, probably took its name from the deep, narrow gorge where prison-like walls of shale and sandstone rise from the dank rock floor.

But the expansion of recreational and economic opportunities did not come without cost. Lake Countians understood that preservation of opportunity, their way of life, and their freedom would not come naturally in a world torn by dissension, and from the beginning they fought in conflicts that raged at all levels—local, national, and worldwide.

Members of the Painesville Cornet Band enlisted in 1861 for a year's duty, then again in 1864 for another nine months of the Civil War. This picture was taken at Lookout Mountain, Tennessee, on October 23, 1864, while the musicians, with several other recruits, served in the Second Brigade, Third Division, Twenty-third Army Corps. During their first tour, they served the Seventh Regiment, Ohio Volunteer Infantry. Courtesy, Western Reserve Historical Society

TIMES OF CONFLICT AND DISSENSION

As the icy blasts of January whistled around the crude log cabins

they called home, Lake County pioneers drew their roughly made

chairs closer to the crackling fire in the hearth as they spun tales

and recounted their experiences. Children, wrapped in quilts and

supposedly asleep in the loft, listened wide-eyed to reminiscences

Proud of their ancestors' participation in the Revolutionary War, the Lake County Chapter of the Daughters of the American Revolution dressed in costume for their Continental Tea Party in 1932. Similar parties were hosted as fundraisers during the Civil War by the Soldier's Aid Society. Courtesy, Lake County Historical Society

of New England boyhoods and the trek west. In some cabins, the stories were probably told by veterans of the Revolutionary War. Christopher Crary may have told of his marine service, including his escape from Halifax Prison and later incarceration on the British prison-ship, the *Jersey*. Eleazar Paine may have thrilled his audience with a drummer boy's view of the war as well as with his father Stephen's adventures in the fight.

Despite the intervening decades, the memories of war still lived in the minds of the early settler who abandoned the ravaged hillsides and coastal towns of New England. As the early settlers trudged towards Lake County in search of a prosperous new life, many never suspected that they would soon face threats of invasion as the conflict between the Americans and the British in Canada escalated into the War of 1812. Defense of the Great Lakes region was crucial and was handled by Generals Van Rensselaer at Niagara and Hull at Detroit. Centered between the two, Cleveland emerged as a rallying point for military activity with hastily erected fortifications and two armed militia companies for lake patrol. "It was a time of great alarm," Christopher Gore Crary later remembered.

In the quiet of an August morning, Captain Nathan Heald led a ragtag band of 67 soldiers and 30 settlers along the lakeshore, carefully keeping between the water's edge and a ridge of sand hills. Their removal from Fort Dearborn on the Chicago River to Fort Detroit had been ordered several weeks earlier by Hull. Less than two miles below the river, 500 Potowatomi and allied Indians attacked. Trapped, the militia charged the ridge, only to be cut down as Indians swarmed the beach, destroying the wagons that contained the women and children. Two women, 12 children, and over 30 men lost their lives in the grisly struggle. The remainder were captured. For the next two days, the Indians celebrated their victory and distributed their prisoners among the various tribes, ignorant that even as they torched Fort Dearborn, Hull surrendered Fort Detroit to invading British forces without firing a shot.

News of battle lost and advancing forces filtered through the countryside. Crary vividly recalled the turmoil in Kirtland:

The Civil War behind them, the patrons of Lake View House settled in for their Independence Day celebration on July 4, 1867. Ancestors of many Lake Countians fought in the Revolutionary War and claimed land in the Western Reserve as part of their military bounties. Courtesy, Western Reserve Historical Society

There seemed to be nothing to prevent the British and Indians from coming down the lake, both by land and water, pillaging, marauding, and destroying everything on the southern shore.

While the women remained at home, carefully covering their fires at night and watching for signs of invasion, their menfolk flocked to Sandusky to make a stand as forces under General Harrison and Colonel Croghan repulsed the enemy at Fort Meigs and Fort Stephenson. The danger had passed temporarily.

That next June part of the British fleet hovered off the Cleveland shore until a thunderstorm drove them away. The Battle of Lake Erie caused further consternation. "We distinctly heard the cannonading," Crary remembered. "The sound seemed to be to the right of Cleveland and a little farther off, and we thought it must be a naval battle. Should the British be victorious, there was nothing to prevent them from landing at Cleveland and ravaging the whole lake shore." Perry's famous message, "We have met the enemy and they are ours," penned from the deck of the *Niagara* on September 10, 1813, took three anxious days to reach outlying settlements in Geauga County and what became Lake County.

As the war wound to a close in 1814, the settlers focused their energies on creating settled communities with the new pioneers

who flocked into the county. Conflict and dissension had not ended, however, as religious and political differences fanned the increasing friction between Gentiles (non-Mormons) and the Church of Jesus Christ of Latter Day Saints (Mormons).

In 1830 Kirtland was a community of agricultural commerce and industry, a frame schoolhouse, and four active religious congregations serving 1,018 people. By the time the New York adherents of Joseph Smith, Jr., migrated into the county in the spring of 1831 over 1,000 of Sidney Rigdon's converts awaited their arrival. A.G. Riddle later wrote:

One almost wondered if the whole world were centering at Kirtland. They came, men, women, and children, in every conceivable manner, some with horses, oxen, and vehicles rough and rude, while others had walked all or part of the distance. The future "City of the Saints" appeared like one besieged. Every available house, shop, hut, or barn was filled to its utmost capacity. Even boxes were roughly extemporized and used for shelter until something more permanent could be secured.

Although Kirtland represented only one stop on the Mormon trek to the true Zion, many Gentiles believed that the entire congregation planned to sink permanent roots into the little community. By 1835 an ornate temple for worship overlooked the east branch of the Chagrin River and a school for teaching the Hebrew language pros-

(Above) The medal which Commander Oliver Hazard Perry received by a resolution of Congress in January of 1814 for his 1813 victory at the Battle of Lake Erie featured his own portrait on the obverse side and, on the reverse side, the U.S. fleet with its 54 guns as it stood out to meet the British fleet. Courtesy, Emelius O. Randall and Daniel J. Ryan's *History of Ohio*, 1911

(Right) "I'm Joseph the Prophet. You've prayed me here. Now, what do you want of me?" Joseph Smith, Jr., is said to have exclaimed upon his arrival at Newell K. Whitney's general store in 1831. After the Mormon flight from Kirtland, the store which is identified here as the post office changed hands several times. It still stands today and has been restored. Courtesy, Western Reserve Historical Society

The Kirtland Temple was meant to be a symbol of stability and respectability as well as a house of worship for the Mormons in the area. Money for the purchase of land and the three-year construction project was donated from members throughout the country while the labor was donated primarily by members of the Kirtland congregation. Courtesy, Western Reserve Historical Society

pered. The Mormons then created their own money-lending institution, the Kirtland Safety Society Anti-Bank, to aid them in their economic endeavors throughout the county.

The *Telegraph* of the 1830s chronicles the Mormon/Gentile mistrust that festered almost from the beginning. The fervency of the Mormon missionary effort caused the initial concern, particularly when converts such as Martin Harris denounced as infidels all who challenged the Mormon Bible. In a Sunday morning sermon, such an announcement might have been overlooked, but coming from the floor of the Painesville Tavern in the middle of the week, Harris' statement caused quite a stir. Spiritual rivalry was further fueled by commercial rivalry. As Crary later remembered:

With means they [Mormons] could have bought every farm in the township. The people all supposed they had got to leave. It was a time of terror. Property was not safe from theft, and many believed that life was not safe with such a crowd, who boasted that they should not hesitate to take life, if the Lord commanded them to do so through the prophet; that they should live off and suck the milk of the Gentiles; that the promise that the saints should inherit the earth was about to be fulfilled, and that they were the saints.

The population of Kirtland tripled in the first six years of the Mormon occupation and by 1837 had outdistanced the combined growth of the communities in Painesville Township. This posed not only an economic threat at a time when, as the county seat, Painesville was desperately seeking to attract population and a major transportation network, but also inevitable political problems. In a county high on nationalistic sentiment, Smith actively declared that God was about to make a "full end of all nations" so that the "real government of God" could be instituted. He further aligned his followers, who voted under his direction as a block, with the Jacksonian Democrats in a county that was predominantly Whig.

Rumors further fueled personal antagonisms. New York examples of Mormon belief in faith healing and their resistance to standard medical practices appeared in area newspapers, inciting concern about public health measures. Especially emotional was the reaction to polygamy, which many believed was actively practiced by the Kirtland Mormons, although present historians have never been able to prove the practice of this belief in Kirtland.

Gentiles found a variety of outlets for their animosity. Eber D. Howe published hostile editorials in the *Telegraph* as supplements to his scathing 1834 publication *Mormonism Un Vailed; or a Faithful Account of That Singular Imposition and Delusion, from Its Rise to the Present Time.* While Grandison Newell, owner of a sawmill and chair factory on the east branch of the Chagrin, denied them employment, consumers rejected Mormon-made products and store owners refused to sell them much-needed grain. Mobs hounded their movement throughout the county and lawsuits plagued Smith, in particular.

With the collapse of their Anti-Bank, which provided them with a medium of exchange that had been sorely lacking, the Mormon community found itself friendless, destitute, and unable to cash in its worthless bills or raise credit. Their solution was to head west. Crary noted that "runners were sent out with pockets full of Mormon money to buy teams where they could find people not posted on the value of Mormon promises to pay. In 1838 the camp was ready to start, and left in a body, making a string of teams more than a mile long." As Mormon William Cahoon lamented, "We turned the key and locked the door of our homes, leaving our property and all we possessed in the hands of enemies and strangers."

And so most of the Mormons moved westward toward their Zion, their abandoned temple an eloquent reminder of their place in Lake County's history. The dust from their passing had barely settled when Lake Countians turned their attention to another controversy, the issue of slavery.

Privately, many area citizens aided runaway slaves on the Underground Railroad. According to folklore, the Painesville-Ravenna Road became known as the Freedom Road, a popular route for fugitives bound from Hudson to the lakeshore, and secret tunnels connected Rider Tavern with nearby homes on Mentor Avenue. Throughout Lake County, blacks found shelter in attics, warehouses, barns, and caves until they could be smuggled to the lake and ships bound for Canada.

Publicly, many citizens promoted abolition societies. As early as 1839 Dr. John Mathews of Painesville strove to unite the societies of Geauga (including Lake), Cuyahoga, and Trumbull counties through the creation of a weekly newspaper to be published in Painesville. Entitled *The Lake Erie Freeman,* the publication aimed to "hold onto the good old 'self-evident truths' of the Declaration of Independence" by promoting certain political issues of the day, including antislavery.

Lake Countians also promoted an antislavery government. On February 16, 1861, just two days before Jefferson Davis was sworn in as president of the Confederate States of America, U.S. President-elect Abraham Lincoln addressed an enthusiastic crowd of 4,000 citizens at the Painesville railroad depot. Many of the students from the Lake Erie Female Seminary attended and, buoyed by the same fervor which swept the rest of the county, launched into preparations for homefront aid to the pending war. In May they raised a flag over College Hall with ceremonial pomp and circumstance calculated to boost patriotic spirits. Over 1,000 townspeople and students sang patriotic tunes, several prominent citizens spoke of the impending conflict, and the Geauga Riflemen performed drills and

Jack Casement adopted Lake County as his permanent home when he met and married Frances Jennings of Painesville while employed by the railroad. Elected major of the Seventh Regiment after the first call to arms of the Civil War, he rose to the rank of colonel, actively recruiting soldiers on the homefront as well as serving in the field. Courtesy, Lake County Historical Society

gun salutes.

The efforts of the seminary students reflected the efforts of citizens throughout the county once war was declared. Perry and Madison women sewed clothing for the soldiers while the students fashioned havelock caps for the Geauga Riflemen and knitted socks for the "poor, weary men" of the Ohio Seventh Regiment. In mid-1862 the seminary students organized their own Soldiers Aid Society as an auxiliary to the Lake County society which collected and shipped food, clothing, medicine, blankets and numerous other supplies to their boys at the front. Lake County's effort was later credited as:

one of the most valued tributaries of the Cleveland Sanitary Commission . . . Its members were unwearied in their work through the whole course of the war, and in addition to their usual supplies were notably active in preparing canned fruit and vegetables and blackberry cordial through the summer months.

Lake County sent more than supplies to the Civil War, it also sent its sons into a conflict that did not end by Christmas, as many had hoped. Fifteen-year-old Hendrick Paine joined the 105th Infantry as a drummer in 1862. Although he was discharged in a year, he later reenlisted for 100 days' service. Many members of the Painesville Cornet Band enlisted as the Band of the Seventh Regiment, Ohio Volunteer Infantry, from June 1861 to July 1862, then again in 1864 with the Second Brigade, Third Division, Twenty-third Army Corps. The band accompanied the brigade through the Hood Campaign from Rome, Georgia, to Clifton, Tennessee, then transferred to Wilmington, North Carolina, where it marched through the pine forests and swamps to Kingston, Goldsboro, and Raleigh.

Carried away on a tide of patriotism and adventure, few dreamed that they were on the brink of one of the bloodiest, most emotional wars in American history. In April 1861 G.W. Northam wrote blithely of his new experiences in a letter to Carmar Kewish.

(Left) While their boys tackled the enemy on foreign shores, Lake Countians pitched in once again to help win the war from the home-front. Victory Gardens appeared, neighbors shared rationed goods, and women went to work in factories. Courtesy, Willoughby Historical Society

We are camped in a cornfield 2 1/2 miles from Annapolis. It is a very pleasant place but I would rather, that is for my part, put up at some good hotel but guess stopping at hotels is played out for a while but there is not use of grumbling. This war is not going to last always . . . even if it should last for fifteen or twenty years we have only [33] months to serve. The boys are all well and in Good Cheer but they do not feel quite so nice as they did when they left Painesville. We were at Cleveland three days. We had some what of a time there, you bet we did.

But the mood changed. By 1864 letters home reflected a more mature and realistic view of the war. As J.J. Greenlee wrote from a camp near Decatur, "Most of the boys is well. I am in good health at this time. There is some complaint among the recruits. They don't stand it like the veterans." Greenlee's "it" included an enforced hike, the prospect of an advance against a large number of rebel troops, and bad weather. "Last week we had a Snow . . . seven inches deep and last night it rained a little and it is very muddy. We have no quarters nor tents since we came back . . . God speed the day when we shall be permitted to live in peace at home."

On November 11, 1918, military authorities finished negotiating an armistice which disarmed Germany, and Lake Countians celebrated the end of World War I, the war to end all wars, with "Peace Day" parades and celebrations such as this one in Willoughby. Courtesy, Willoughby Historical Society

Lake County cemeteries and village monuments vividly remind us that many did not return home in 1865 to enjoy the peace that followed the painful reuniting of the nation.

On the eve of the twentieth century, the Spanish American War anticipated a new age of increased conflict and dissension. On July 6, 1898, Finnish immigrants from Fairport joined native Lake Countians in answering the call to arms when Company M marched from the armory to the train depot, accompanied by the citizens' band and members of the Grand Army of the Republic. The *Telegraph* later reported:

It was difficult to decide which received the greatest ovation—the veterans who have already served their country at the front or the new and untried company of young men who are going to face the hardships of another war.

Although the war was brief, it set a pattern that Lake Countians would follow several times over the next century. While their boys

went off to war, families at home buckled down to aid the war effort. During both World War I and World War II, this often meant financial investment in war bonds, doing without luxuries such as sugar, and volunteer service in the age-old arts of sewing and knitting for the boys overseas. Service flags waved from windows overlooking front yard Victory Gardens full of vegetables. The prevailing idea was that food would help win the war and everyone pitched in to overcome the manpower shortage that plagued the farms as well as industry. During World War I, city girls stationed at Lake Erie College donned khaki knickers and the title "Farmerettes" as they stacked wheat and gathered berries throughout the county.

Industries modified their production to fulfill the changing needs of the war machine, often completely changing the products they manufactured. Lake Countians still whisper about the top-secret activities at barbed wire-enclosed companies such as the Ben Hur plant in Willoughby where Lewisite, a deadly methyl gas, was manufactured for use against the German Army in World War I. During World War II, defense plants such as Industrial Rayon, Ohio Rubber, and Diamond Magnesium geared up to 12-hour work days and seven-day work weeks, the second shift often worked by high

While farmers and nurserymen were at war, the Farmerettes of Lake Erie College pitched in to fill the shortage of labor created by World War I. Children took on extra chores, parents purchased war bonds, neighbors shared luxuries, such as sugar, and Victory Vegetable Gardens sprang up in front yards instead of flower patches. Courtesy, Lake Erie College Archives

school students and teachers. Hiring practices also altered as women answered the call for labor.

Although World War II ended in 1945, newspaper headlines and letters postmarked from foreign lands continued to plague Lake Countians throughout the Korean Conflict from 1950 to 1953 and then throughout the Vietnam War. Although the county's war monuments were originally dedicated to the soldiers and sailors of specific wars, they represent poignant memorials to all who served in behalf of their home and a way of life that was not always peaceful, not even in peace time.

Twentieth-century Lake County found itself increasingly linked to conflicts that raged nationwide. The prohibition/temperance argument was older than Lake County itself. Distilleries flourished in the days of pioneer industry, turning surplus grain into a product that could be easily stored, transported, and exchanged for other goods. In his reminiscences of pioneer days, Crary related numerous anecdotes involving alcohol in Kirtland, suggesting that:

Whisky was cheap, and could be obtained for labor or most any kind of produce; no temperance society had ever been heard of . . . and many excuses could

Industries throughout Lake County changed their production focus to aid war efforts throughout the twentieth century. During World War I the Penfield plant in Willoughby switched from the manufacture of tile, brick, and drain tile machinery to the production of shells. Courtesy, Willoughby Historical Society

be made for the early settlers. They had left good homes, with the conveniences and comforts of civilization, and placed themselves here in the woods, with neighbors few and far between, with but few of the comforts of life; with the lean task of hewing out a farm from the dense forests, and the long years it must take to obtain a comfortable home; it seemed to them to require something to stimulate and nerve them for the task, and give them courage to face the battle of life which was before them.

By the 1830s many Lake Countians bemoaned the evils of drink and took steps to moderate its use. At the first annual meeting of the Kirtland Temperance Society, the membership voted to purchase the nearest distillery under the agreement that it would never be used as a distillery again. The actual vote does not survive today, but 239 people signed their names to the society's constitution. By 1899 prohibition had become a political question in Kirtland and the community voted 167 against 31 for a "dry" township. Twenty years later, township opinion was reinforced on the national level by the Volstead Act, which outlawed the manufacture, sale, transportation, and possession of intoxicating beverages. For the producers of fruits for wines and hard cider the economic impact promised to be severe, but was mitigated by the rampant bootlegging and whisky-running that developed in retaliation.

Fairport became a bootlegger's paradise with its easy access to both Cleveland and Canada via the lake. By 1921 concerned citizens decided that the time had come to clean up their small town and that the person for the job was Dr. Amy Kaukonen.

A daughter of Finnish immigrants, Kaukonen was born in Elyria, Ohio, in February 1891, graduated from Conneaut High School as valedictorian of her class, and attended the Women's Medical College of Pennsylvania at Philadelphia at the age of 17. About 1920 she and her mother moved to Fairport where Kaukonen set up a thriving medical practice until a citizens' committee requested that she head the reform ticket as a mayoral candidate. Conducting her own campaign, she promised to wage war on the whisky-runners and bootleggers, winning the election and becoming one of the first women mayors in the United States. Her election attracted the attention of the *Lady's Home Companion,* New York newspapers, and the local news media, who delighted in the seeming paradox of a petite young blonde with a broad smile, sharp mind, and a reputation for toughness. Unblinded by the spotlight, Mayor Kaukonen tackled her campaign promises, often leading the liquor raids with the help of Fairport officials and state prohibition authorities from Cleveland. In 1923 the *Plain Dealer* reported that "Ever since she assumed the reins of the local government, there has been constant excitement in the tiny village." Photographers and reporters attended most of the trials at the village hall, a small wooden structure that "seldom was able to accommodate the many kibitzers when the lady held court." A stern judge, her usual fine for bootleg cases was $1,000 plus costs.

In the midst of Kaukonen's term, B.F. Harris resumed the mayoral post and Dr. Amy Kaukonen slipped away from Fairport. Reports of her whereabouts conflicted, although it seems likely that she moved to Seattle, Washington, to head a women's hospital. Perhaps her decision was nothing more than a good career move, but many Lake Countians still whisper that once, while she was receiving patients, two armed men appeared in her office. Certainly a stand against the bootleggers and whisky-runners made many a prime target for foul play until the Volstead Act was swept away by the 21st Amendment and President Roosevelt's measures for recovery from the Great Depression.

Failing industry, falling prices for agricultural products, and general unemployment marked the 1930s. Because so many Lake Countians were tied to the land, conditions were less harsh than in urban areas. Farm families often aided relatives by providing foodstuffs, township and county funds helped needy families, and the Lake County Relief Committee distributed free seeds for Relief Gardens. Lifestyles returned to the basics of an earlier age as people "made do" with what they had. In November of 1934, Sadie Talbot Eddy of Willoughby wrote in her diary that she had "Finished weaving stair carpet. Lacked rags for last 1/2 yard . . . I tried to color rags to finish rug." Sadie's diaries illustrate the energy and richness of life in Lake County, despite the Depression. In addition to her baking, mending, cleaning, and gardening, Sadie actively involved herself in church and social activities such as the Bookworm Club, Music Club, W.C.T.U., and Ladies Aid Society. For recreation she quilted with her friends, listened to Charlie McCarthy on the radio, and enjoyed the simple pleasures of nature and her neighbors. If she wanted to go out over the weekend, famous bands such as Kaye Kaiser's performed in the township parks. The beaches came alive during the hot hours of the afternoon with swimming, and during the balmy nights as people settled down on picnic benches to watch free movies and munch on popcorn and hotdogs.

But even as Lake Countians pulled together to fight the effects of the Depression, the forces of unionization began pulling them apart. In 1936 a violent strike at the Ohio Rubber Company heralded the arrival of unionism. The National Guard manned machine guns from the rooftop as protection for the armed management employees who reported to work. Similar episodes followed at other Lake County industrial sites, including Diamond Alkali, before the Congress of Industrial Organizations was finally accepted. By the 1960s unionism was accepted by both management and la-

During World War II Lake County soldiers served in foreign countries and on faraway seas as they joined all branches of the armed services. Those in the Navy served on ships such as the U.S.S. *Augustus*. At home factories once again converted to war production, consumer goods were rationed, and facing shortage became a way of life from 1941-1945. Courtesy, Willoughby Historical Society

borers and 95 percent of the county's work force belonged to either United Mine Workers or the AFL-CIO.

Countless other social issues divided Lake County over the next several decades, one of the most recent and pressing being the Perry Nuclear Plant.

Just before lunch on a cold Friday in January 1986, the great horned owls in the Lake Metroparks Wildlife Rehabilitation Center in Kirtland began aggressively clacking their beaks. Usually a measure to frighten other animals, this was a sign of agitation and impending danger. At 11:47 A.M., Lake County began to shake. Furnace explosion? Airplane crash? Semitrucks hitting the building? Speculations ran wild, but the most frightening, and perhaps the most prevalent, was—Perry Nuclear Plant? Phone lines jammed as calls flooded into police stations. Within moments the word was out about the Lake County earthquake of 1986. The experience was not soon forgotten. Everyone had a story about what they thought it was, where they were,

what had happened to them, and those stories were still circulating a year later, despite the minimal damage caused by a 30-second jolt that registered 4.96 on the Richter scale.

The earthquake has passed and most of the broken windows have been repaired, but concern over what could have happened had the Perry facility been operational at the time has not faded. Although subsequent inspections of the power plant determined minimal structural damage, county commissioners and concerned citizen groups throughout Northeastern Ohio expressed fresh dismay over the incident and the possible inadequacy of proposed emergency evacuation plans. Today, headlines concerning local plant shutdowns and discussions of building a low-level radioactive waste-disposal facility in Ohio continue to appear in county newspapers and fuel the dissent over the Perry Nuclear Power Plant. Issues such as these highlight the challenges of building "community" in the ever-changing world of the 1980s.

Water-powered mills such as this one flourished along the rivers and streams of early Lake County as the frontier era waned and the pioneer economy matured. While the farmers ground their wheat into flour at local gristmills, nearby sawmills turned rough logs into clapboards for the building of frame-houses, and workers in the woolen mills readied sheep's wool for spinning and weaving. Courtesy, Lake County Historical Society

BUILDING COMMUNITY

"Ralph Granger, from Canandaigua, New York, located at Fairport about 1820. His natural and acquired abilities were exceedingly good. As a classical scholar, and for general and varied knowledge, he had no peer, probably, on the Reserve," stated the authors of the *1880 Pioneer and General History of Geauga County, Ohio.* Granger, as Fairport historian Helen Kasari has further noted, was a lawyer with diverse interests that led him into service for his new community in the Geauga County Agricultural Society, Willoughby Medical College, Ohio Senate, and possibly the mayoral seat of Fairport Village. He was not, however, unique to the early settlers of Lake County, many of whom devoted countless hours to the establish-

At the instigation of professionals and citizens alike, educational institutions like the Madison Seminary sprang up throughout the county. When its enrollment dwindled, the buildings and grounds were donated to the National Woman's Relief Corp for the Soldiers' and Sailors' Home. In the late 1950s the Ohio State Department of Mental Health and Hygiene took over the property. Courtesy, Western Reserve Historical Society

ment of schools, churches, and organizations while actively practicing their professions.

Like Granger, many Lake County professionals turned to politics during their careers, including Chagrin (now Willoughby) lawyer David Abbott, whose political career included terms as sheriff, representative to the Ohio Constitutional Convention, Ohio state representative, Ohio state senator, and presidential elector for the Fourth District of Ohio. His Constitutional Convention colleague Samuel Huntington served his community not only as supervisor of roads and justice of the peace, but also in the Ohio state senate, state supreme court, and the governor's seat, while early teacher Abraham Tappen of Madison later became an associate county judge.

The examples of these men and others like them were followed by later area politicians such as James Abram Garfield, who moved to a farm in Mentor in 1876. By that time, the Cuyahoga-born Garfield was already well known throughout the Western Reserve. Educated at the Geauga Seminary in Chester and the Western Reserve Eclectic Institute at Hiram (now Hiram College), he later taught and then served as president of his alma mater before entering politics. After serving two years as an Ohio senator, he actively joined in the Civil War, becoming the youngest major general in the Northern Army before his military service was interrupted by his 1863 election to the United States House of Representatives. Seventeen years later he embarked on his famous "front porch campaign" for the presidency of the United States, which he conducted largely from the wide front porch the Garfields had added when enlarging their farmhouse several years earlier. A small outbuilding was converted into campaign headquarters and connected to the larger world by a telegraph line. The Lake Shore Railroad ran excursion trains through the area and arranged a special stop at a cow lane leading to Garfield's farm, dubbed "Lawnfield" by the press. But Garfield's presidential victory was short-lived. He died in September of 1881 from a gunshot wound inflicted by a disappointed office seeker several months earlier. As a biographer would later lament, "Broken short as it was, his career has that completeness that inheres in a life lived consistently and unflinchingly in the light of reason and kindness." Part of that completeness certainly included community spirit and service.

But lawyers and teachers were not the only professionals who held such values. In addition to their frequent struggles against nature, disease, and the common health complaints of everyday life, doctors were active throughout the Lake County community. Chagrin physicians John Henderson and George Card were the principal founders of the Willoughby University of Lake Erie, appropriately taking special interest in the medical college. Dr. John Mathews, an early resident of Painesville, was particularly active in the abolition movement, while his colleague Dr. Storm Rosa devoted considerable time and effort to education in his position as president of the Painesville Education Society.

For all their contributions, however, the professionals of Lake County have never been solely responsible for the building of their community, but have shared the burden with a citizenry intimately

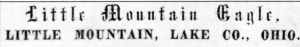

This House is open for the reception of pleasure seekers and invalids during the summer season. The location is too well known to need description. Its wild and romantic scenery, cool invigorating breezes, pure water, fragrant pines, and shaded

WALKS AND DRIVES

render it by far the most healthful and delightful place of resort in Ohio. THE LITTLE MOUNTAIN EAGLE Is decidedly the best finished and best furnished house on the Mountain, and is especially adapted to families or to those desiring the quiet and the comforts of a home. It is a few rods beyond Stocking's Tavern, and pleasantly situated.

LITTLE MOUNTAIN is six miles from Willoughby Station, on the Cleveland and Erie Railroad. On arriving at said station hacks will be in readiness to take passengers to the Mountain on reasonable terms, as per agreement.

This place was originally designed as a Water Cure, and a good physician might successfully carry out the original design without interfering with the arrangements for summer company, and the proprietor is ready to receive a partner with a capital of a few thousand dollars or to sell out, as he wishes to retire from business.

Terms of Board and Lodging by the week, $12.00; by the meal, 75 cts. Good stabling for horses.

The interests of Dr. Storm Rosa ranged widely from his community involvement with the Painesville Education Society, Willoughby Medical College, and Geauga County Agricultural Society to his development of the Little Mountain Watercure, which is reputed to have operated a few years before William S. Gardiner converted it into a hotel, the Little Mountain Eagle. Courtesy, Lake County Historical Society

tied to their roots and traditions. Through their combined efforts such institutions as the Mentor Library Company, formed in 1819 and serving the county for 40 years, mushroomed into over three dozen libraries serving today's population. Membership in a large variety of organizations peaked and waned as interests and concerns shifted over the years. The popularity of the abolition societies lasted through the Civil War, later to be replaced by the temperance societies of the late nineteenth century. By 1934 Sadie Talbot Eddy of Willoughby was actively involved in the Bookworm, Music, and Miscellany clubs as well as the Women's Christian Temperance Union and Ladies Aid Society. Had she chosen to, she also could have become involved with the fledgling Lake County Historical Society which was founded in 1936. At that time the society had a dual purpose: to operate Lawnfield as a museum and to collect, preserve, interpret, and exhibit Lake County's past. By the mid-1980s, that purpose narrowed to exclude the operation of Lawnfield when the site was purchased by the National Park Service, and the historical society sought new quarters to develop a comprehensive resource center for Lake County history. The range of other organizations and activities available for

At Lake County's 1940 Centennial Celebration the young Roc-kerrettes performed to rousing music for the crowd's entertainment. Musical celebration had long been a part of the Lake County tradition from that first Fourth of July when a fife and drum band led the procession from the Paine to Walworth homes. Courtesy, Lake County Historical Society

Lake Countians also expanded over those 50 years to include service clubs, some national and some local, and professional support organizations such as the Western Reserve Writers and the Business and Professional Women's Club. For those interested in the performing arts, Lakeland Community College offered vocal, instrumental, and dance opportunities.

Lake Countians banded together musically throughout their history. At the first Fourth of July celebration held at John Walworth's home, "the people who had already assembled under the bower in front of the cabin, were agreeably surprised by the approaching and soul-stirring sound of martial music." This impromptu fife and drum band was just a forerunner of the music organizations that sprang up throughout the county. Both Madison and Mentor had early singing schools and Madison boasted the first band in the county. Years later the Painesville Cornet Band celebrated the laying of the cornerstone of the Lake Erie Female Seminary and accompanied Lake County recruits to the Civil War.

Perhaps one of the longest lasting types of organizations were those based in agriculture. Lake Countians played an active role

In 1924 the members of the Madison Glee Club stepped in time to colonial music. Glee Clubs were just one popular choice among many for Lake Countians looking for organized recreation in the twentieth century. Courtesy, Madison Historical Society

The Painesville Cornet Band, a voluntary musical organization, played at the opening of the Cowles House Hotel in 1857. Courtesy, Lake County Historical Society.

in the Geauga County Agricultural Society from its formation in 1823 until they created their own society in 1852. In that year they purchased Painesville property for a fairgrounds in anticipation of an annual fair to encourage competition and education in agriculture. Just over 20 years later several Granges, officially known as the Patrons of Husbandry, formed in townships throughout the county with the help of Anson Bartlett of North Madison, who also worked on the organization's national policy. After the turn of the century, the Lake County Farm Bureau was formed as a branch of the Ohio Farm Bureau Federation and continues today, with the Grange, to operate actively on behalf of Lake County's agriculture.

The growth of the Granges and Farm Bureau was accompanied by the steady growth of 4-H Club work after the 1929 Wall Street crash. According to a *Madison Press* summary of the 1935 annual report of the Lake County Agricultural Extension Offices, 4-H had grown steadily from only one organized boys' club in 1929 to a 1935 enrollment of 147 boys in 10 clubs. Six years earlier, the projects had been limited to potatoes and vegetables but by the mid-1930s they ranged from potatoes, vegetables, and poultry to specialty crops such as raspberries, strawberries, corn, and tomatoes, and agricultural engineering.

Twentieth-century agricultural production continued to be a viable part of the local economy and today county production is in excess of $20 million, even though the centers of activity have changed. Herds of black and white Holstein dairy cows once so popular have dwindled, and the nurseries and orchards which once flourished in the central and western portions of the county have moved into eastern townships such as Perry and Madison to avoid the suburban sprawl. This illustrates what some have described as the two opposite orientations of county development. Communities east of the Chagrin River maintained ties towards an agrarian lifestyle much longer than those west of the river, who gravitated toward the urbanization and industrialization of metropolitan Cleveland. Today, travelers on Route 2 and Route 20 can easily observe such development in their passage from one end of the county to the other.

Diversity within the county is also suggested by a look at the county's population since the Progressive Era. At the western end of the county, the concentration of Italian-American families traces its roots and traditions back to the turn of the century and the theory that Wickliffe resident Harry Coulby imported Italian laborers to work on his villa, now the Wickliffe City Hall. A similar surfeit of work and lack of labor encouraged the immigration of several Eastern European groups into Fairport after the harbor was revived through the construction of new docks, and after the replacement of the narrow-gauge railroad with a standard gauge by Pittsburgh capitalists. The first Finns, Hungarians, and Slovaks trickled into Fairport in the 1880s, but full-scale immigration did not peak until after 1900. Religious diversity accompanied such immigration, and new churches appeared on the Lake County landscape. While the Finns established the Zion Lutheran, Immanuel Lutheran, and First Evangelical Lutheran churches, the Hungarians, Slovaks, and

New construction and development has changed the face of Lake County. Most of the frontage within the county has been converted into residential property, although there are still a few places in the eastern townships where human habitation is not visible as far as the eye can see. Courtesy, Madison Historical society

other Roman Catholics formed the St. Anthony's and St. Michael's Greek Catholic churches.

Population diversity also manifested itself in the festivals offered throughout the county. Today, in addition to the traditional Lake County Fair held each August, Fairport Harbor sponsors its Mardi Gras in early July and features the ethnic foods and dancing of its Eastern European heritage. In late July the Little Mountain Folk Festival, hosted by the Lake County Historical Society, celebrates the county's traditions with a weekend of folk music and dancing, arts and crafts, and ethnic and traditional foods. Appropriately, the festival is held at the Lake County History Center located at Shadybrook Farm on Little Mountain. The setting itself celebrates an important period in the county's heritage, a time when the wealthy of Cleveland chose Lake County for their summer homes. Shadybrook Farm, the summer home of the Arthur D. Baldwin family, was established in the early twentieth century as a working farm of 543 acres and three tenant farm families. When the original house burned in 1925 it was replaced with the current structure. In 1955 the Baldwin heirs sold the farm to Holden Arboretum, which incorporated most of the acreage into its planting and management programs while renting the house to a Laymen's Retreat Association. In 1984 the Lake County Historical Society negotiated a long-term lease with the arboretum for the occupancy and development of its history center at Shadybrook. By preserving the house and surrounding 14 acres, the Lake County Historical Society has provided its visitors with a glimpse of a bygone era in which formal gardens, intricate stone grape arbors, and a polo field in the meadow represent favorite leisure activities of the gentlemen farmers and country estates which dotted so much of Lake County.

The ridge in Wickliffe was the first to be developed into summer estates for Cleveland industrialists in the 1890s, but as transportation improved, the trend spread through Waite Hill, Mentor, and Kirtland

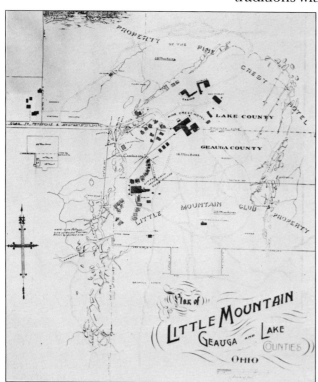

Many families of Cleveland industrialists banded together in the late 1870s to form the Little Mountain Club. By 1920 the social activities of the club had ceased and many of the members began buying up the countryside for summer homes. It was just east of the Little Mountain Club property that the Baldwin family established Shadybrook Farm. Courtesy, Lake County Historical Society

to encompass what had once been the resort hotels on Little Mountain. Although most of these estates exist today only in pictures, remnants of a few can be seen as one drives the twisting roads of the Kirtland Hills.

Far back on the Lakeland Community College campus, the mansion of Cleveland industrialist Edward Moore sits, awaiting possible preservation. Moore's property, called "Mooreland," once extended from what is now Route 306 east to Garfield Road and from the East Branch of the Chagrin in Kirtland north to Mentor Avenue. Lakeland bought a chunk of the property for its campus from Moore's daughter and, although the mansion itself has not been preserved for use, the daughter's honeymoon cottage houses the college's Physical Plant staff. On campus it is known as "Camelot." Similarly, Leodoro, the estate of Moore's partner Henry Everitt, is known today as the Kirtland Country Club, and Lantern Court, a Georgian Colonial home built in the 1930s, is a featured part of Holden Arboretum surrounded by formal gardens and murmuring streams.

Concern over the preservation of Lake County's historic and natural heritage has encouraged citizens throughout the county to band together in their efforts. The Lake County Chapter of the Archaeological Society of Ohio staffs its own Indian Museum in Kilcawley Hall on the Lake Erie College campus. An outgrowth of the work the archaeological society members were doing at local sites, the initial purpose of the one-room museum was to preserve prehistoric Indian artifacts of the surrounding areas and display examples of arts and crafts from the entire North American continent. Today the museum not only offers displays which are revised every six months and often include special exhibits from other institutions and private collections, but also maintains a small library for research and hosts group tours, lectures, and workshops. People of all ages—Scouts, senior citizens, as well as college students—have visited for lectures, research, and to view the exhibits.

While the Indian Museum provides Lake Countians with a special classroom on prehistoric man, Holden Arboretum and Lake Metroparks provide them with a glimpse of their natural heritage

Christmas is a traditional time of year to bring the tangy scent of fresh pine indoors and Holden Arboretum aids in the effort by offering Christmas crafts workshops where children learn wreath-making. Holden's quarterly class schedules reflect the changing of the seasons and the elements that make each a special time for Lake Countians. Courtesy, Holden Arboretum

that often links up with local history. Hikes led by knowledgeable guides onto the Holden Arboretum holdings of Little Mountain inevitably combine lectures on the world of plants and trees with insights into why the saddleback formation became one of the region's most prominent resorts. Further linkages between natural and historic heritage will be forged by the Lake Metroparks' plans for expansion, which include the development of a historic working farm.

Of course the preservation of history itself has become a tradition in Lake County as can be seen by the development of numerous community historical societies, such as those in Willoughby, Leroy, and Wickliffe, which complement the work being done on the county level. One of the oldest of these is the Fairport Harbor Historical Society, formed in the 1940s in an effort to renew the Fairport Lighthouse and keeper's quarters as a marine museum, which it operates to this day. Another historic site opened by community effort was the Little Red Schoolhouse, now located near the Willoughby-Eastlake Board of Education. Committed to creating a museum in which today's students could learn to appreciate their heritage through participation in historic learning situations, the entire community pitched in to help. The Willoughby Village Council loaned funds while businessmen, residents, and organizations donated their time,

Lake County is a wonderful place for winter sports, especially when they are combined with an educational experience. Holden Arboretum offers children an opportunity to learn snowshoeing while enjoying nature in a season often overlooked for recreation. Courtesy, Holden Arboretum

skills, equipment, and materials toward the renovation of the Harvey Hall School, which was originally built in 1901. In 1975 the brick schoolhouse was moved from Euclid Avenue to its present location on Shankland Road and two years later opening ceremonies were held.

A year after the Little Red Schoolhouse opened, the Madison Historical Society formed to preserve its community history. Its development eventually led to its acquisition of one of the historic homes near the village square, where it operates a craft shop and opened a museum in the spring of 1987.

Other institutions have become involved in the preservation of Lake County history in the 1980s. Lake Erie College created its own archives for the preservation of its own history as well as that of its forerunner, Willoughby Female Seminary, in 1980. Morley Library in Painesville expanded its facilities to include a special Local History and Genealogy Room staffed by volunteers from the Lake County Genealogical Society.

Through efforts such as these, Lake Countians have attempted to reconcile their past with their present as they face the future. Certainly, their quest to preserve their traditions is most understandable in light of the changing landscape around them. Perhaps our answers lie in where and what the county has been for its people since its birth almost 150 years ago.

PARTNERS IN PROGRESS

Lake County's early forests furnished a wealth of game to its hunters, and later stocked the early fur trading posts. Its great stands of timber the settlers sold at profit while clearing their lands. This timber supported sawmills, charcoal furnaces, asheries for making potash, tanneries, forges that smelted iron, and smithies that shaped the iron.

Lake County's rivers and streams powered gristmills to grind the settlers' grains. The lumber from its sawmills built homes, wagons, roads, ships, and factories. Then, as the largest trees disappeared, sawmills gave way to factories making baskets, boxes, spools, furniture, and staves for barrels, tubs, and pails.

Clearings for family subsistence quickly evolved into specialty agriculture. The lake effect shielded farms from drastic temperature swings, protecting against withering late-spring frosts and lengthening the fall harvest season. Local farms yielded peaches, plums, grapes, berries, and vegetables for area tables. Dairies produced milk, butter, and cheese.

The area soon became a center for nurseries that stocked not only Lake County's orchards but also those of the surrounding counties and states. Lake County grew into the nursery capital of the world, supporting more than 200 nurseries in its heyday. With time, suburbs have encroached into farmlands, and many nurseries have migrated eastward, from the Mentor-Painesville area to the Perry-Madison area.

The growth of industrial Cleveland next door had a far-reaching influence. The railroads that connected Cleveland to markets east and west also linked Lake County. The rise of the automotive industry spurred the growth of parts and materials suppliers throughout the region.

Increasingly in the 1940s and 1950s, Lake County saw a westward drift of Cleveland companies seeking cheaper land for expansive new factories. With the construction of Interstates 2 and 90 centered around the railway tracks starting in the 1960s, a wide industrial belt took shape.

Over the years Lake County's economy has grown more and more regional—having a wider sphere of influence and at the same time becoming more susceptible to outside influence. Today its industries compete within a national and increasingly international arena.

The population supported by the economic expansion in Lake County and to the west has spurred the growth of housing developments and commercial centers. Residents have seen their county change from a string of sleepy towns bordered by farms into one sprawling megalopolis.

Lake County's present economy very much depends on the skill and acumen of its resident companies. Many of them have done very well through the grit and ingenuity of their founders, successors, and employees. The pioneering spirit of its settlers is now found in its businesses.

The organizations whose stories appear on the following pages helped to support this literary and civic project celebrating the sesquicentennial. They illustrate the variety of ways in which individuals and their businesses have contributed to Lake County's growth and development. The civic involvement of such businesses, hospitals, and other local institutions, in cooperation with its citizens, has helped make Lake County an excellent place to live and work.

LAKE COUNTY HISTORICAL SOCIETY

For a community to have a strong sense of identity, it must have an appreciation of its history. The Lake County Historical Society, now in its second half-century, has played a major role in preserving and interpreting the local past for area residents.

The organization was founded in February 1936 with a dual purpose: to collect, preserve, interpret, and exhibit items from Lake County's past, and to operate Lawnfield, the James A. Garfield home, as a museum open to the public. The society undertook both full-time tasks, incorporating as a nonprofit organization in 1956 and adding other worthwhile projects over the years.

In the 1960s the society focused on programs to commemorate local and community history. To increase awareness of Lake County's rich heritage, the society initiated a Heritage Home program to document, register, and recognize with plaques important structures. To date, more than 200 structures have been recorded, and other localities have looked to this program as a model.

In 1978 the Lake County Historical Society established an Education

Department to coordinate and interpret holdings. Its first program, Pioneer School, has given more than 5,000 elementary school students from five Northeast Ohio counties a hands-on feel for life on the northeastern Ohio frontier. The Ohio Association of Historical Societies and Museums named it the state's best educational program in 1981.

Three years later the society followed up with its award-winning Continuing Education Series, which offers lectures, workshops, and seminars on such topics as President Garfield's role in the Civil War, Painesville's lost landmarks, and making and playing the dulcimer. In 1985 the association cosponsored with Lake Erie College a popular two-day symposium on Western Reserve regional history and culture.

After Congress designated Lawnfield as a national historic site in 1980, the National Park Service became Lawnfield's steward. The society began looking for new headquarters and found it in Shadybrook House, a federal revival mansion on a 14-acre property acquired from the Holden Arboretum. Shadybrook House had been the summer residence of the family of Rebecca Williams Baldwin and Arthur D. Baldwin, grandson of pioneering Hawaiian missionaries.

The Little Mountain Folk Festival, an annual midsummer celebration hosted by the society, offers traditional American and ethnic folk arts, music, crafts, and dance.

The organization soon began rehabilitating the structure, developing it as the Lake County History Center. It also moved two log structures to the site and erected a replica one-room schoolhouse and craft barn. In May 1984 the society opened to the public the History Center, with its exhibits and extensive library of books, documents, maps, photographs, and microfilms.

Looking ahead, the society plans to continue hosting special programs such as the annual Little Mountain Folk Festival, as well as symposia and workshops on area history and culture. It publishes a bimonthly newsletter, a history magazine called *Lake County Historical Quarterly,* and sponsors special publications, such as *Here Is Lake County* and this volume. It will work to expand museum space to permit exhibits of larger scope and help coordinate the celebration of Lake County's sesquicentennial in 1990.

In the past and in the future, the Lake County Historical Society's accomplishments are made possible through the cooperation and generous support of Lake County residents.

Opening a door to the past—the Cobb-Burridge House during disassembly. The structure, which once stood next to Mentor High School, dates back to 1840, the county's founding year. The Greek revival structure will expand exhibit space when reerected at the Lake County History Center.

OHIO BROACH & MACHINE COMPANY

"Broaching is a high-production cutting process used to shape metal or plastics," says Charles P. Van De Motter, president and chairman of the board of Ohio Broach & Machine Company. "It's a very specialized technology, but one that is used in just about every industry, including consumer goods, automotive, aircraft, defense, and agriculture."

Seeing the potential for broaching early and eager to be in business on their own, Van De Motter, his father, Charles J., and two partners started the company and officially opened for business on January 1, 1957. They designed, manufactured, and reconditioned broaches—the jagged tools that cut the surfaces they move across. They worked out of the Van De Motter garage at 645 East 125th Street in Cleveland.

In 1959 the Van De Motters bought their partners' share of the business. Two years later the firm moved to larger facilities at 399 East 131st Street in Cleveland. About that time the company began rebuilding broaching equipment. It entered the production broaching business when the Grubiss Company sold Ohio Broach its broaching equipment.

Ohio Broach faced a difficult turning point in 1962. To establish itself in its new production business, the company gave 48 percent of its stock to Frank Zagar of Zagar Inc. in return for Zagar's sideline broach business, financial assistance, and valuable consultation. By 1964 Ohio Broach had turned around and bought back its stock.

After building Zagar's broaching machines for a few years, Ohio Broach engineers in 1966 designed their own machine. It was small but considerably faster and more rugged. In 1971 the company began manufacturing a high-speed vertical broach machine that was 2.5 times faster than its predecessors.

Another technical feat soon fol-

Founder Charles P. Van De Motter's garage was the original site of Ohio Broach & Machine Company. Today the company has more than 70 employees and occupies this 37,000-square-foot facility in Willoughby.

lowed: tying the high-speed machines into automation to load and eject parts. Equipment size also grew, culminating in a 50-ton, 80-inch-stroke, vertical pull-down machine used to manufacture Abrams M1 tank parts.

Small or large, just about every Ohio Broach order is unique. The client presents a prototype part and asks for a machine that will cut and contour that part to specifications. Then Ohio Broach employees work hand in hand with the client from the custom design of the machine and tooling, to training the machine operators and start-up.

The rapid growth of Ohio Broach & Machine Company is largely due to the talent and hard work of its employees. Through their skill, they produce broaching machines and tooling that can cut parts rapidly and precisely. Through their efforts, the firm is attuned to new developments in electronics and computer numerically controlled (CNC) equipment.

Growing demand for the firm's products led to its move in 1974 to

Broaching is a cutting process used to shape metal or plastics, and Ohio Broach & Machine manufactures the equipment to do it. Here an employee operates a surface broaching machine, which broaches both cutting edges on various-size rotary lawnmower blades.

a 20,000-square-foot plant in Willoughby. This facility, expanded by 17,000 square feet in 1984, is completely full today.

Currently Ohio Broach & Machine Company has more than 70 employees who handle between $5 million and $6 million in annual sales. The only full-service broach company in Ohio, the firm's orders come from across the country, from companies such as General Electric, Colt Industries, and Chrysler Corporation, and also from foreign countries, including France, the Philippines, and South Korea.

DAVIS FUNERAL HOME

Founded in 1905 by L.P. Davis, Davis Funeral Home is the oldest continuing funeral home established in Lake County and the oldest business in Willoughby still operating under the same name.

Davis began his business in the Austin Building on Erie Street with a "new Sayers and Scovill hearse, a casket wagon, a good team and harness, and a stock of caskets." He had attended Adelbert College of Western Reserve University in Cleveland and received his professional diploma from the Massachusetts Embalming School in Columbus in 1904.

During the formative years of his business, Davis taught high school, taking S.D. Shankland's classes when the Ohio legislature met. In 1906 he married Jessie Langshaw, who became his helpmate in his profession. Jessie was granted her own funeral director's license in the 1930s for her practical experience.

At the constant mercy of weather, Davis and an assistant survived one particularly treacherous trip to Montville—a distance of about 18 miles—that lasted from 11 a.m. to 8:30 p.m. the next day. Davis recalled "taking turns hanging off the seat of the hearse to keep it upright in the

snow" and arriving with "our clothes frozen stiff from the wet snow, which soon froze to us." Such trips inspired him in 1914 to buy the first auto ambulance in the three-county area—a Packard.

When a burial was scheduled for Lake View Cemetery, Davis sometimes hired out a special railway hearse car from The Cleveland Railway. "It had a compartment in front divided from the passenger seats," he recalled. "This took care of the family and friends who wanted to go to the cemetery. Lake View Cemetery had a track laid into the grounds so the car could be switched inside."

In 1914 Davis moved his business down Erie Street to the Cleveland Trust Building and added a line of furniture. Back then, nearly every funeral director needed another source of income—most often a furniture store or a livery stable.

At the end of World War I the business was moved from an office to a home at 37812 (once 49) Second Street. Prior to that time, remains were prepared in the deceased's residence. Now such work was done in the funeral home, and the family could schedule services for either the funeral home or church.

Davis' son, Roger V., earned his diploma from the Cleveland School of Embalming in 1928 and joined the family business. In March 1932

L.P. Davis, funeral home founder, teacher, and historian.

Roger married, and his wife, Frances, a registered nurse, began assisting him in the business. That April the present home at 4154 (once 36) Clark Avenue was purchased, and Davis Funeral Home moved to its present location.

A growing business soon created the need for more staff. In 1948 Howard W. Taylor joined the firm and completed 34 years of service before his retirement in 1982.

L.P. Davis retired in 1959 and the firm was acquired by his son, Roger. In 1967 L.P.'s grandson, Charles R., graduated from Cincinnati College of Mortuary Science and joined the family firm along with his college classmate John R. Vaughan. In 1979 Charles became the third generation of the Davis family to own and operate Davis Funeral Home.

Over the years the staff of Davis Funeral Home has grown to four licensed funeral directors/embalmers, plus other employees, but the philosophy of L.P. Davis still applies. "No person can operate a successful business alone. He must have loyal friends, and we have been so fortunate to have made many in our years. These we value more than any material gain we may have had."

The Davis Funeral Home ambulance with L.P. Davis at the reins in 1907, when funeral directors customarily volunteered ambulance service to their communities.

TELEDYNE OSTER

To join pipes so they carry liquids without leakage first demands precisely cut threads. Cutting such threads requires highly specialized, exacting machinery—the kind pioneered, manufactured, and refined by Teledyne Oster for close to a century.

When the company was founded by Herman Oster in December 1893, pipe threading was a laborious job done with simple hand tools. Oster pioneered the application of power, first using overhead belts and then electric motors. He also invented a hammer-chuck to hold pipes firmly in place, and used multiple chaser threads to speed the cutting. With the new machines a worker could cut six threads in an hour instead of in a day, so Oster's business thrived.

Within a decade the firm outgrew its first location, a one-story frame workshop on East 40th Street in Cleveland, and moved to 2057 East 61st Street. It merged with Williams Tool Corporation of Erie, Pennsylvania, in 1929 to offer full lines of both power pipe and bolt threading equipment.

During World War II Oster's machines threaded thousands of miles

of pipe to deliver water to servicemen and fuel to aircraft, tanks, and jeeps. After the war the company introduced innovations such as the automatic opening die head and a single set of threading dies that could cover the range from 2.5 inches to eight inches. The increased productivity of Oster's machines boosted the nation's plumbing, heating, and electrical contracting industries, as well as its chemical, petroleum, and other industries.

In the mid-1950s, facing a growing worldwide demand, the firm's dynamic owner, Roger B. Tewksbury, and other executives built a state-of-the-art plant and offices at its present Wickliffe address. In 1962 Tewksbury sold the business, which had been family owned for more than 50 years,

A 1974 Teledyne Oster sales seminar held at the plant in Wickliffe.

to a group of five outside investors. Seven years later these investors sold the company to Landis Machine at the same time Landis was acquired by Teledyne, a California firm.

Today Teledyne Oster offers the widest assortment of stationary and portable pipe and bolt threading machines in the world. Its dedicated factory craftsmen also build a pipe roll grooving machine, a roller pipe cutting machine, and a complete line of threading dies. Recent innovations include a special formula thread cutting oil that dissipates heat as it is created and a portable machine with a splash-proof reservoir. Looking ahead, Teledyne Oster engineers are developing new uses for existing equipment, especially in advanced factory production systems.

To appreciate the requirement for perfect threads, consider the skill needed to build machines that cut American Petroleum Institute standard threads. These threads are the only thing holding miles of pipe together to extract crude oil from deep wells.

Teledyne Oster has been in the threading business longer than any other company. Justly proud of this achievement, the people of Teledyne Oster remain dedicated to staying in the lead in threading.

An early electrically powered threading machine made by Oster in the 1920s.

LAKE HOSPITAL SYSTEM, INC.

Lake Hospital System, Inc., maintains a healthy balance between the old and the new by keeping alive a sense of history and its long ties to the community, and by offering patients the latest in technique and technology.

The system's earliest roots go back to 1834, when a state charter sanctioned the creation of Willoughby Medical College. The institution supplied much-needed physicians for the area, but unfortunate disagreements among its faculty caused it to disband by 1847. Four faculty members left for Cleveland to found what would become the Case Western Reserve University School of Medicine, and the rest moved to Columbus to found what now is The Ohio State University College of Medicine.

Lake County's first chartered hospital opened in July 1904 in Painesville through the sponsorship of the New Connecticut Chapter of the Daughters of the American Revolution (DAR). During its first three decades, Painesville Hospital provided care for patients who were typically very ill. Horse-drawn ambulances brought in patients, who often had to be carried upstairs on stretchers by staff in the days before elevators.

In the 1930s the national movement to make physician training more consistent and vigorous spread to Ohio, though home baby delivery was still the rule. During the Depression Painesville Hospital was turned over to the county commissioners as Lake County Memorial Hospital.

Antibiotic treatment and regular emergency room service began in the 1940s at Lake County Memorial Hospital. Back then its physicians reported an average of three or four emergencies per 24-hour shift. In the 1950s hospital personnel became increasingly skilled and specialized. As a result, the use of student nurses for general care declined, and with it the training program for nurses.

Meanwhile, Willoughby residents felt a growing need for a hospital of their own. In the mid-1950s local physicians and businessmen spearheaded a drive to convince the Lake County commissioners of this need. The effort was successful, and Lake County Memorial Hospital West opened its doors in 1961.

The 1960s and 1970s saw an ex-

Chris Niederkorn, R.N., monitors a newborn infant's heart rate. The child is in an isolette receiving photo therapy for jaundice, consequently, the protective covering over the eyes.

Painesville Hospital, forerunner of Lake Hospital East, soon after its opening in 1904. Housed in the Stephen Mathews House on Washington Street, it was said to occupy one of the most attractive spots in the city. This house was one of several designed by noted Western Reserve architect Jonathan Goldsmith.

plosion of new technology, as well as tremendous expansion in facilities and staff at both hospitals to provide more sophisticated services.

In the 1980s the medical advances continue, but with increased emphasis on personalized care and reaching out to the community. For example, one nurse is chiefly responsible for the 24-hour care of one patient from admission through recovery in the hospitals' primary nursing program, and mothers-to-be can now choose home-like birthing rooms. Preventive health care is coming of age, supported by an array of community outreach and education programs, and active sponsorship of support groups. In addition, there are fully equipped and staffed emergency trauma rooms at both institutions, as well as urgent care centers in Mentor and Willowick.

Today Lake Hospital System, Inc., has a combined capacity of 359 beds, a medical staff of more than 350, and a support staff of 1,900 that includes 600 volunteers. Its men and women have the expertise, technology, and facilities to provide treatment in most areas of medicine. For complex illnesses they work as a team to hold multidisciplinary clinics for patients' convenience and to decide jointly on the best course of care.

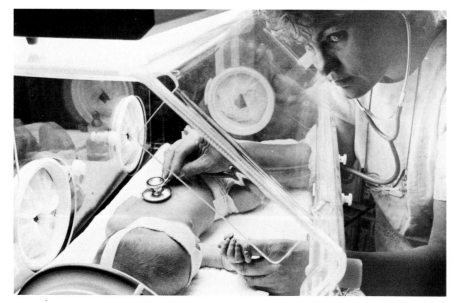

TRANSCON INCORPORATED

Transcon Incorporated designs, builds, and contracts miles of conveyor systems for applications ranging from light manufacturing to major automotive and scrap handling. In fact, Transcon is one of the nation's top firms in the manufacture of steel belt conveyors.

John Musial and Don Parshall, now deceased, started the company in 1958. Musial, now president, recalls that establishing the business really took a decade.

Through their efforts came expertise, satisfied customers, and growth. In 1961 Transcon built a plant at its present site on Twinbrook Road, which was a major step in keeping better track of the long and involved manufacturing process. Transcon had farmers and nursery owners for its neighbors.

That same year the company adopted the name Transcon. An advertising agency helped pull the name together, noting that the firm manufactured both "trans"ferring machines and "con"veyors.

Since its construction the plant has expanded four times. Currently the complex contains 47,000 square feet of manufacturing and office space. Inside the plant, employees do their own stamping, and then machine and weld the steel sheet, plate, castings, and other components into products.

Transcon supplies conveyors from four inches to 12 feet in width and as long as needed. The firm's products can be found in many automotive plants, including more than two miles of steel belt conveyor each in General Motors' Mansfield expansion and Lordstown stamping plant, and in Chrysler's Sterling stamping plant. Overall, Transcon specializes in conveyors and equipment for the

One of the foremost manufacturers of steel belt conveyors, Transcon builds conveyor systems ranging from light manufacturing to major automotive and scrap handling.

metalworking industries—machine tool builders and the steel, aluminum, and copper industries. The largest conveyors can be found in steel mills, and the company has built some of the world's largest steel belt scrap handling systems.

Though Transcon has serviced some industries that have been shrinking in recent years, it has managed to maintain steady growth. The firm has diversified into systems to handle solid wastes for municipalities and builds a variety of special applications.

Today more than half of Transcon's business is outside of Ohio, and 10 percent is foreign. However, its Lake County location continues to be central for its suppliers and customers. Though the firm uses regional distributors, all of its key sales engineers work out of the Mentor office, Transcon's sole location.

Because just about every order involves custom work, completing a job

John Musial, president.

takes a real team effort, lots of on-the-job training in engineering and management, and attention to details. In a sense, everyone at Transcon Incorporated is an essential link in building its products and in the firm's success.

Transcon Incorporated's Twinbrook Road headquarters in Mentor.

OHIO RUBBER COMPANY

These days rubber companies don't just make rubber products. They compound a family of rubbery substances called elastomers that are as versatile as plastics. Therefore, Ohio Rubber could easily be called International Elastomers—especially now that its scope has expanded to cover millions of products for hundreds of industries worldwide.

The firm first took shape in 1874 as the Cleveland Rubber Company, a jobber and merchandiser of rubber products founded by John McClymonds, president of Ohio National Bank, and his brother L.K. The firm, then located at 8 South Water Street, made suction hose for breweries, garden hose, washer wringers, belting, packing, tubing, car and machinery springs, valves, gaskets, and other rubber accessories.

In 1893 Ohio Rubber was formally incorporated. Two years later the firm united with Cleveland Rubber Company, becoming Ohio's largest distributor of mechanical rubber goods, including rubber clothing, belts, shoes, and fire hose.

By 1903 the thriving Ohio Rubber opened a Cincinnati branch. Henry Hallock managed the new branch and later went on to serve as company president from 1911 to 1932. Expansion continued with a

An Ohio Rubber Company delivery truck, circa 1939.

move to larger facilities on St. Clair Avenue in 1906 and the purchase of Detroit's Mechanical Rubber Company in 1913.

A technological breakthrough in 1923 spurred the firm's evolution as a major auto supplier. Budd Bronson, an Ohio Rubber Company employee, discovered a way to make rubber running boards using presses and adhering them to a metal base. To exploit this profitable innovation, the corporation acquired the old Buckeye Rubber Company facilities—nine acres and 75,000 square feet of floor space—now Ohio Rubber's headquarters site on Ben Hur Avenue in Willoughby.

A front view of a running board press.

In 1929 Chevrolet bought Ohio Rubber's entire production of running boards. Ford Motor Company also became a customer and Goodrich a licensee, making the firm the largest employer in Willoughby.

Ohio Rubber stayed resilient during the Great Depression, providing steadier employment than most organizations and beginning product diversification programs. Franklin Smith led the company through the difficult 1930s, the war production years, then back to a peacetime economy. During World War II employees worked three-shift days to produce diving masks, life belts, surf boats, aircraft drop tanks, fuel cells, and tank tracks. After the war Ohio Rubber built a plant in California so it could sell to a burgeoning West Coast market.

In 1951 General Herman Safford began eight years of service as president. The following year Ohio Rubber was bought by Cincinnati's Eagle-Picher Company, a leader in mining and refining lead and zinc that was founded in 1843. At the time the firm had 1,500 employees, an an-

LEFT: Mats are trimmed on an Adamson punch press.

BELOW LEFT: These tank tracks produced at Ohio Rubber wait at the railroad siding for shipment during World War II.

nual payroll of more than $7 million, and a production surpassing its war-time peak.

Under the Eagle-Picher banner, Ohio Rubber's growth continued. In 1957 it acquired Gora-Lee Company in Stratford, Connecticut. Two years later Ohio Rubber built a plant in Arkansas.

The 1960s saw keen competition and adjustment, with plants closing in California and Arkansas by 1965. Then Philip McManus became president and steered the corporation away from an overreliance on mass-produced goods toward engineering solutions to uncommon problems. Ohio Rubber's new mission was to satisfy customers' design and performance needs with elastomers and other materials formed into custom shapes. At its Willoughby laboratory, researchers developed a host of new elastomer-based products through joint engineering with businesses in aerospace, mass transit, and other industries.

In the early 1970s Ohio Rubber, under John Painter's leadership, was decentralized into autonomous divisions. Each division reported to the Willoughby headquarters, but had its own manufacturing, marketing, engineering, and financial staffs. The decentralization was a success, and new plants went up around the country to apply Ohio Rubber's research breakthroughs. Painter became an Eagle-Picher group vice-president, and Joseph Kiernan succeeded him as president.

Ohio Rubber Company employees celebrated the firm's centennial over three days in 1974. It started its second century on a sure track, working as a team with customers in the product planning stage and taking increased responsibility for quality control. In the mid-1980s it established a European operation and sold the last of its divisions that made more standard industrial products. Today the Willoughby headquarters provides guidance and control to high-tech divisions and operations nationwide and overseas.

The people of the Mat Division and Willoughby Services Division keep the Willoughby plant humming. The Willoughby Services Division compounds high-performance materials for a vast range of industry applications, one of the more demanding being windshield wipers for jet aircraft. The core business of the Mat Division is interior trim materials for the automotive industry—cars, light and large trucks, and specialty automobiles.

There was a time when a car mat was just a flat covering to protect the metal floor. But through the ingenuity of people in the Mat Division, a mat now also serves as a sound barrier, thermal insulator, and color-coordinated, textured, interior-design element. To design and vacuum form these three-dimensional mats involves the close cooperation of scientists, engineers, artists, and production people.

Because of the division's technical prowess, its has become a leading U.S. supplier of vehicle floor coverings. Its products have won a prestigious Q1 quality rating from Ford and also the patronage of GM, Chrysler, and American Motors.

Ohio Rubber's other divisions make more than one billion parts annually, all to customer specifications.

In Paris, Illinois, the Injection Molding Division creates rubber automotive and industrial components through an injection process, once thought only applicable to plastics.

In Denton, Texas, the Orthane Division turns out highly engineered parts from polyurethane, a material that combines the elasticity of rubber with the toughness of plastic.

In Norwich and Stratford, Connecticut, the Orcomatic Division turns out millions of parts per day on the company's patented high-speed molding wheels. The process creates parts that are uniform enough for automated assembly. This technology was used to build a new Eagle-Picher operation, with plants in West Germany and Spain. Its head, Andries Ruijssenaars, is the newest Ohio Rubber president.

More and more, rubber and plastics materials are growing closer together, and the Ohio Rubber Company is a leader in bridging the gap.

MENTOR LUMBER AND SUPPLY COMPANY

By far the largest lumber company in Lake County, Mentor Lumber and Supply Company has deep local roots reaching back to the 1920s. Its current owner-managers have served home owners and professional builders at Mentor Lumber since 1963, and now similarly serve many of these customers' children and grandchildren.

Mentor Lumber was incorporated September 20, 1922, with a stock issue of $15,000. Its first owners were T.P. Kirby, president; his brother, S.M. Kirby; and John Hillenbrand.

In its first year the company did $98,316 worth of business from a building at Hart Street and the Nickel Plate Railroad. Later the owners built at 7180 North Center Street, its current Mentor address. More land was acquired by these and other owners.

To balance its seasonal lumber business, Mentor Lumber sold coal in the winter and builders' supplies, such as concrete block and sewer pipe. In fact, it sold more coal and builders' supplies than lumber in its first four decades.

The current owners bought Mentor Lumber on November 1, 1963, and focused on lumber. The partners in the purchase were Jerome Osborne (chairman), Harry Fishleigh (president), and Robert Sanderson (secretary)—friends with extensive experience in the lumber business. They saw a growing demand for lumber in Mentor and agreed that a locally owned and run lumber store would be a community asset.

Three older buildings containing mostly outdated equipment came with the purchase, so the new owners plowed back early profits into modernization. In the mid-1960s they purchased 17 additional acres and labor-saving lift equipment. "Can you imagine? When we started here we hand unloaded and loaded all incoming and outgoing deliveries," says Fishleigh. "Now we have six lift trucks to facilitate this handling."

During the 1960s and 1970s six new buildings were added to the Mentor location. These new structures were not just warehouses but also included a 10,000-square-foot home center. This retail expansion was opened in 1972 shortly after the completion of the Route 615 railroad overpass. Additional yards were opened and enlarged in Madison and Chardon.

The volume of business done by Mentor Lumber in its first year of operation under its new owners is now surpassed monthly. The number of different items in stock has multiplied to 30,000. These volume increases necessitated the installation of a computer system. This installation was overseen by the newest corporate officer, assistant secretary, and president's son, Harry Fishleigh III. This system handles point of sale, accounts receivable, and the accounting functions.

The number of employees has increased from 7 to 70, but all still know each other by first name. "We work with a good group of peo-

A mid-1980s view of the Mentor complex. In 1987 another large warehouse was constructed.

ple," reflects Harry Fishleigh, Jr. "There are few formalities, and no one is hung up on titles and positions."

Business is still booming from the first of April to the end of November, but now some spills into the colder months thanks to do-it-yourselfers.

Busy or not, many folks at Mentor Lumber still find time to be active within their communities. A few have served on boards. Fishleigh sat for 15 years on the Mentor Planning Commission, and Donald "Pete" Davidson (company treasurer, stockholder, and retail manager) has served on the Kirtland City Council.

These volunteer efforts accentuate the two-way relationship that Mentor Lumber and Supply Company has strived to obtain with its community. This relationship has resulted in Mentor Lumber, through its products and reputation, becoming a part of many Lake County residents' daily lives.

PERFECTION CORPORATION

If you own a water heater, chances are that its fittings and drain valve came from Perfection Corporation of Madison, Ohio. And if you own a natural gas-equipped home, Perfection fittings connect the service line to your meter set.

In 1944 Samuel Jacobson bought a small pipe nipple manufacturing business in Cleveland. He kept its "Perfection" name, but moved it the following year to Madison due to the wartime labor shortage in the Cleveland area. His colleagues, Frank Blair and Ralph Passerell, stayed with the company, and today offspring of all three families are prominent among the firm's 200 employees.

The company's first major diversification began in the late 1950s. According to Ray Emigh, vice-president/ sales and marketing, a sales agent spotted a copper-lined steel fitting made for water heaters and recommended entering that market with a brass-plated fitting for longer life.

Soon I.D. "Budd" Jacobson suggested lining the fitting with plastic for even greater economy and life. Over time plastic-lined fittings from Perfection's Fabricated Products Division became common components in the water heating and appliance industries. Today plastic-lined fittings are the second-biggest contributor, after glass-lined tanks, for extending water heater life.

In the early 1960s the firm introduced a plastic-lined drain valve for water heaters and soon after introduced an all-plastic model, selling many millions of them to date.

In 1972 Perfection expanded into gas distribution products. The company patented its plastic-insulated risers, stiffeners to reinforce plastic pipe, and other products. Later a joint research program with Consolidated Natural Gas resulted in an alternative to the heat fusion process for making plastic pipe connections. Researchers developed fail-safe stab fit-

Perfection Corporation's past chairmen of the board: Sam Jacobson (top left), Herman Jacobson (top right), I.D. "Budd" Jacobson (bottom left), with the current chairman, David Jacobson (bottom right).

tings (based on the principle of a Chinese finger toy) that greatly reduced installation costs.

Through its outstanding safety record, expertise in plastic injection molding, and statistical process control, the firm has lived up to its name. Perfection is regarded as number one in its field and is well represented on various national standards committees in the gas distribution and appliance industries.

Locally both Perfection and its employees actively support their communities. "Our employees play key roles locally and often win awards for creative fund raising," says Nancy Jacobson, a third-generation employee and board member. "As an example, our annual spaghetti dinners aid the United Way over and beyond individual and company contributions. Our

good-neighbor policy means relying on local vendors whenever possible and pursuing ventures with local partners."

Today Perfection Corporation operates plants in Madison, Geneva, and Harpersfield, plus one in California, and licenses Alcan Canada Ltd. to manufacture for Canada and Europe. "A future orientation is a tradition here," says David Jacobson, chairman of the board. "We're looking ahead with professionals, like our president Joe Gregory, to guide our operations, and investing in research and engineering to stay on the leading edge of our industry."

NORTHEASTERN OHIO GENERAL HOSPITAL

Northeastern Ohio General Hospital officially opened to the public in August 1959. The private, nonprofit institution was built in North Madison through six years of extraordinary effort by two osteopathic physicians, Dr. Jessie Hutchinson of Geneva and Dr. Joseph Lefler of Painesville.

A grateful patient's gift of $20,000 in 1953 to Dr. Hutchinson sparked the dream. She and Dr. Lefler, stretched thin by a heavy case load, wanted to build an osteopathic hospital to attract colleagues and also provide much-needed hospital services to the northeast area. That October, with Dr. Charles Stull of Geneva, they incorporated the hospital, then formed a board of trustees of prominent area citizens. Before going ahead with the project, Dr. Lefler rang doorbells across Madison, asking residents if they wanted a hospital; they answered, "Yes."

Through much work and despite many setbacks, the doctors and board members somehow met all federal requirements, resolved all construction problems (such as quicksand on the building site), and financed the 28-bed hospital at a cost of $570,000.

After six years of struggle by Dr. Jessie Hutchinson and Dr. Joseph Lefler, Northeastern Ohio General Hospital opened its doors to the public in 1959. This photo was taken one year later.

Seniors from the area are invited to the hospital the first Monday of each month to have a nutritious lunch and hear a presentation of health information by a staff physician.

Once in operation the facility drew many compliments on its care and friendly, personal atmosphere. Some say its warmth stems from its small size and rural location. Others attribute it to the spirit instilled by its founders, volunteers, employees, and board, which includes people from all walks of life. Still others find its roots in the holistic approach of osteopathic training, which teaches physicians not only diagnosis and treatment of disease but also emphasizes the relationship between the muscles, joints, bones, and other body systems.

The hospital's popularity led to an addition of 20 beds in 1969 and the construction of the 32-bed Hutchinson-Lefler Wing in 1976. With the added space came the Physical Therapy Department, the Nuclear Scanning Division in the Radiology Department, an updated laboratory, pharmacy, laundry facilities, Community Room, and, lately, the Genesis Unit for the care of alcohol and drug abusers.

Northeastern Ohio General has looked beyond its walls in recent years, actively inviting the community inside and bringing care out to the community. Extra support for many outreach programs comes from the Jessie-Rose Marie Guild of volunteers, in-service volunteers, and Candy Stripers.

As part of the Senior Monday Program, seniors from the surrounding area meet at the hospital the first Monday of each month to have a tasty, nutritious lunch and hear a presentation of health information. The hospital also has delivered care, such as lab tests, direct to nursing homes. It has opened physician-staffed offices in Perry and Fairport Harbor and created Twenty-Forty One, Inc., a subsidiary providing Northeast Ambulance Service, Chapeldale Pharmacy, and Fairport Pharmacy to the public.

Today about 45 staff doctors— both D.O.s and M.D.s—and other hospital staff provide general hospital care to patients from throughout the Tri-County area. For more complex problems, such as cardiac surgery and serious burns, the doctors refer patients to specialized institutions, if necessary utilizing Life Flight helicopters to airlift patients for speedier care.

THE COE MANUFACTURING COMPANY

Rooted in Painesville for 136 years, The Coe Manufacturing Company has played an important role in building America. It has long been a leader in the plywood machinery industry.

In the mid-1800s the forests of Lake County supported forges, asheries, tanneries, sawmills, and wood products plants. Amid this activity Harold Coe and Leonard Anderson founded the company in 1851 as "manufacturers of steam engines, machinery, sawmill, shop, and grist-mill engines."

As area forests dwindled, loggers moved on, but the partners stayed. They designed the rotary lathe in 1859, so mills supplied with trees unfit for boards could make baskets, spools, barrel staves, pails, and veneer.

In 1870 local interests asked the firm, now owned by Coe and Fredric Wilkes, to make thin wood tapers for lighting gas lamps. The result was a rotary cutter veneer machine and clipper that peeled a sheet of veneer from a log and sliced it into long toothpicks.

In 1891 Coe, then a respected Painesville mayor, bought out Wilkes and gave the firm its present name. However, the country entered a long depression in 1902, Coe died six years later, and World War I saw Coe's plants commandeered to make shell-turning lathes.

The firm fell into receivership in 1919. But within a year a gifted engineer named Frank Milbourn saw its promise. He assumed a large mortgage, dusted off the worn factory,

LEFT: Model 72 Coe veneer dryer.

BELOW: Coe headquarters and plants in Painesville.

and brought in talented salesmen and engineers. His team revamped Coe's veneer dryers and lathes for making plywood, and sold them across the continent and around the world. They also designed new board dryers for the fiberboard and gypsum-board industries.

Coe survived the Great Depression by making steam traps. Its contributions to World War II included steam traps for Navy ships, veneer machinery for making plywood, and dryers for drying synthetic rubber.

In the postwar years the firm shipped loads of plywood machinery and developed various machines to streamline plywood and gypsum-board production. Its major developments in the 1960s were a new jet veneer dryer that halved drying time, log chargers, and a complete equipment line. As the pine plywood industry took root later in the South and the fir industry grew in the Northwest, Coe built a plant (1960) in Tigard, Oregon, and opened an office (1967) in Georgia.

With Potlatch of Lewiston, Idaho, Coe developed the X-Y lathe charger in the mid-1970s. This device married mechanical, electrical, hydraulic, and optical technology with a computer, allowing efficient use of every log.

In 1977 Frank Milbourn's son, Frank Milbourn, Jr., president since 1957, and grandsons, Frank III and George, sold Coe to Fred Fields, former head of western operations. Under Fields' strong engineering and management leadership, the firm has made many acquisitions and is adapting advanced plywood technology to the sawmill industry.

Today The Coe Manufacturing Company's letterhead describes its business as "Lumber, Plywood, Composition Board, and Gypsum Wallboard Machinery." Behind that statement is a history filled with leaders and employees of courage, perseverance, and vision.

AVERY INTERNATIONAL (FASSON)

Like double-faced tape, the Avery story has two sides: being a leader in the industry it founded, and its reputation of being a good place to work. The company is known for pressure-sensitive products, which range from product and address labels and bumper stickers to reflective stop signs, bandages that apply drugs, fasteners for disposable diapers, and tapes that bond rooftops onto cars. It's also known for sensitivity to employees and the surrounding environment.

The story begins in 1935 in a tiny loft in Los Angeles, where R. Stanton Avery made the world's first self-adhesive labels mounted on protective backing. With his invention, Avery created not only a business but also an entire industry.

A rare hybrid, Avery combined a technical wizard with a people person. He could formulate the first synthetic pressure-sensitive adhesives and design the machinery for manufacturing self-adhesive labels; at the same time his warmth and charisma could foster creativity and enthusiasm in his people.

By the 1950s sales passed the million-dollar mark, and the firm expanded beyond its Pasadena headquarters. In 1953 Avery built a new plant in Painesville. The town was picked because it stood halfway between the major markets of New York and Chicago, and it was on a main rail route.

Operations started up, and the Fasson Division was soon established to manufacture pressure-sensitive, adhesive-coated papers, films, foils, and foams. Major expansion or additions to the firm's manufacturing, research, office, or warehouse facilities in Lake County—and outside Ohio—followed about once every two years through the 1980s.

Managing this incredible growth through the 1960s and 1970s was William "Bill" Dodge, a vice-president and general manager who always kept a personal touch. Known as "Mr. Fasson," Dodge interviewed every new employee in the early days, knew every employee by name, and personally wished each employee a happy holiday at year's end.

Today about 1,200 employees work in the area for two groups. It's no longer possible to know everyone by name, but managers make an attempt to know as many as possible.

The Materials Group (U.S.), headquartered on Auburn Road in Concord, oversees five major divisions: two in Indiana, one in Canada, and two in Lake County. Its Lake County divisions include Fasson Roll Division, which is also headquartered in Concord, and Fasson Specialty Division, which is headquartered on Chester Street in Painesville and has a plant on Hardy Road in Painesville and a new plant on Heisley Road and Route 2 in Mentor. The Materials Group also oversees plants in California, Florida, Georgia, Ohio, Pennsylvania, Indiana, Kansas, Texas, and Ontario, Canada. Its distribution and finishing facilities are in New Jersey and Texas.

The Materials Group headquarters of Avery International (Fasson) on Auburn Road, Concord.

The Specialty Tapes Division, headquartered and with a plant on Chester Street, also has a plant off Route 615 in Mentor.

To make labels in its plants, the company buys huge rolls of paper or other materials, up to 80 inches wide. These rolls are placed in machines about three stories high, the length of a football field, and a little wider than the widest paper. In the machine, lacquer is applied on a liner (backing) paper, which is then cured in an oven. Meanwhile, adhesives are applied on foil, film, paper, and other materials and cured. Next the rolls are laminated together and sent to slitters, which slice them into smaller rolls. These rolls are sold to converter companies that print and cut the rolls into labels or other products.

This process deals with wet and dry chemicals, resins, and rubbers that can generate plenty of polluting dust. But Avery people pride themselves on keeping a clean atmosphere inside and outside. Their compliance in cleansing emissions and their development of safer chemical adhesive systems have won them environmental awards.

Avery takes special pains to keep employees informed of events and involved in decision making. Communication is two way, promotions are from within whenever possible, and training is extensive.

Strong company concern continues to this day. The firm offers competitive wages and ample benefits. It sponsors wellness programs and maintains a 25-acre park in Madison for employees and their families and company events. Inside are a pavilion, tennis courts, and children's playgrounds built by employees with materials supplied by Avery. Whenever possible, employees' children are given summer jobs.

The firm also sponsors a full list of activities—golf, softball, skeetshooting, skiing, and bowling leagues and outings; a chorus; Christmas parties for employees; and Christmas and Halloween parties for workers' children.

Making all this possible is a high level of quality and productivity, and a constant stream of successful products, many of which did not exist 10 years ago. Avery taps the ingenuity of its technical specialists, including chemists, engineers, and biologists.

Avery innovations can be found everywhere. Avery people pioneered the easy-removal silicone coating on backing papers, crack-and-peel backing, and stronger backing material that permits faster labeling of everything from pickles to shampoo and reduces manufacturing costs. They developed the first banana labels, closure systems for diapers—including new refastening designs—and porous medical adhesives that allow air and water vapor to pass for the wearer's comfort.

For the automotive industry Avery researchers created ultrastrong adhesives that withstand drastic temperature changes, vivid orange labeling material for slow-moving vehicles, and striping, textured films, and glitter strips used for decorating autos and boats.

With steadily expanding product offerings and sales, and a reputation for good working conditions, Avery is known as a company that's on a roll.

The 25-acre Fassonation Park was created by Avery employees with materials supplied by the company. It is maintained by Avery for the enjoyment of the employees and their families and for company events.

QUAIL HOLLOW RESORT

No wild quail live on the grounds, but the name fits the rustic resort and conference center well enough that nobody questions it. The resort sits on 700 acres of rolling countryside, much of it virgin forest.

Concord's Quail Hollow Resort, the only resort in Lake County, was started by Cleveland developer Milan Kapel and his brother Frank. They purchased the site after learning the right-of-way for Interstate 90. In mid-1965 the first spade of soil was turned to build a 100-room motel with outdoor pool and attached restaurant. Kapel designed the restaurant so that the stage could be enjoyed from both the separate bar and dining room with banquet and meeting rooms.

First named Tanglewood, the motel opened for business on Memorial Day 1966, hosting as its first guests star center John Havlicek and his new bride, and the rest of the championship Ohio State University

A typical Quail Hollow guest room.

basketball team. Kapel operated the restaurant as one of the first Brown Derby franchises in Ohio. Hence, a 15-foot-high statue of a bull stood guard outside. Two years later Kapel renamed the motel Concord Motor Inn and the restaurant Paul Revere Restaurant.

In 1971 three investors purchased a three-quarters share of the inn along with the surrounding acre-

Quail Hollow's championship golf course was designed by Bruce Devlin, a nationally known golf pro, and Robert Von Hagge.

age. They had ambitious plans to complete it as a luxury resort. Inside they remodeled the inn and constructed an indoor pool, whirlpool, and saunas. They added locker rooms, a golf shop, and grill room, and also began building an additional 70 guest rooms. They also hired Bruce Devlin, a nationally known golf pro, and Robert Von Hagge to design a championship golf course.

One investor, architect Dick Van Auken, is credited with designing the additions and naming the resort. He was sitting on the back porch one day when the words "Quail Hollow" came to him. Later the rooms throughout the inn were named after game birds and country themes, and quail appeared on the menu. The dining room became the Quail Wagon, referring to a plantation tradition of having a royally appointed mule-drawn wagon bring the niceties of life to gentleman hunters on their back-country trips.

In 1974 money became tight, construction halted, and the resort changed hands. It was operated first by Ramada Inns and then by Trans-

Designed by architect Dick Van Auken, Quail Hollow's circular indoor pool is available to guests even in the most inclement weather.

america Hospitality. Diamond Shamrock Corporation purchased the complex in October 1976.

Diamond Shamrock retained the staff and renovated the dining rooms and guest rooms, completed the last nine holes of the par-72 golf course, and hired a superintendent and golf professional. Bill Bricker, then Diamond's chairman, added a personal touch by displaying his mounted deer and other hunting trophies on the premises.

In the years that followed the staff grew and continued to serve both the public and the corporation. By 1978 the resort earned a Mobil three-star rating and a AAA three-diamond rating. In 1983 Club Corporation of America, a professional club management company that manages more than 200 country clubs and resorts nationwide, began operating Quail Hollow Resort.

Lois Fultz, director of sales and marketing and the employee with the longest tenure, recalls a number of prominent visitors at Quail Hollow. Entertainers such as Tanya Tucker, Mickey Gilley, and the late Ricky Nelson have been guests at the resort; Waylon Jennings even performed at the facility. Other notables who have spent a night include Olympic Gold Medalist Jesse Owens, Congressman Dennis Eckart, Maureen Reagan, the municipal and common pleas judges of Ohio, and the Cleveland Browns.

Today Quail Hollow Resort attracts people from a 200-mile radius and annually hosts more than 2,000 special events, 254,000 meals, 41,000 room nights, and 28,000 rounds of golf. Local companies such as Lubrizol, Avery, Standard Oil, and B.F. Goodrich hold meetings, seminars, and retreats in the center's 14 meeting rooms. Organizations such as Lake County's United Way, Big Brothers, Big Sisters, Boy Scouts of America, and the Mentor Chamber of Commerce have held golf tournaments. In 1981 Quail Hollow hosted the Coors Open on its course. Area residents have celebrated countless weddings, anniversaries, and birthday parties, and have even held a cotillion ball there.

"At times people call us at the last minute, but we somehow manage to pull some rooms out of the air," says Fultz of the resort's close-knit staff of 200. The record-setter, she recalls, was making arrangements in just four hours for an emergency meeting and party for 500 Bank One guests.

Unquestionably the busiest season is summer, a time of clam bakes, barbecues, hay rides, and other activities. Summer resort guests play tennis on lighted courts, hike on eight miles of nature trails, work out on the outdoor exercise trail or in the indoor fitness center, golf, and swim or, when the snow covers the golf course, enjoy cross-country skiing.

Joseph Lucko, Quail Hollow general manager and past president of the Greater Cleveland Hotel Association, observes that guests feel relaxed and secluded, even though the resort is a half-hour from the heart of Cleveland. Another paradox is that Quail Hollow Resort looks very isolated, but has close ties with the community. Lucko himself is active in the Painesville Area Chamber of Commerce, Lake County Development Council, United Way, Rotary Club, and the Ohio Hotel and Motel Association. So the hosts keep busy, the guests have a good time, and no one misses the quail.

Dining is an elegant event in the Quail Wagon Restaurant.

THE CLEVELAND ELECTRIC ILLUMINATING COMPANY

From an airplane flying over Lake County on a clear night, you can see the county's growth and development charted by clusters of lights dotting interstates and the lakeshore. Electric energy has fueled the growth of Lake County and the rest of Northeast Ohio. Providing that energy has been the job of The Cleveland Electric Illuminating Company (CEI) since the dawn of the electric age.

On the night of April 29, 1879, a switch was thrown and 12 electric arc lamps illuminated Cleveland's Public Square. This was the first electric street lighting in America. Staging the event was Clevelander Charles Brush, inventor of the electric arc light and founder of the Brush Electric Light & Power Company, a forerunner of CEI.

The Cleveland Electric Illuminating Company began business in 1881. By the turn of the century CEI service was expanding throughout Cuyahoga County. In the 1920s CEI's own system expansion and its acquisition of 36 private or municipal utilities extended the company's service to Lake, Geauga, and Ashtabula counties. Municipal customers who had been paying as much as 12 cents per kilowatt hour enjoyed CEI's maximum rate of five cents per kilowatt hour.

In the 1930s CEI acquired no territory, but its annual residential sales doubled in the 10-year period ending in 1939. During World War II Northeast Ohio was one of the nation's biggest wartime producers. Power demands soared. CEI met them.

As the war drew to a close, CEI took steps to ensure a vigorous peacetime economy by forming an Area Development Department, the first of its kind in the nation. Professional salesmen from the department actively promoted the business and industrial advantages of Northeast Ohio to the rest of the nation. Reinforced by other organizations, CEI helped at-

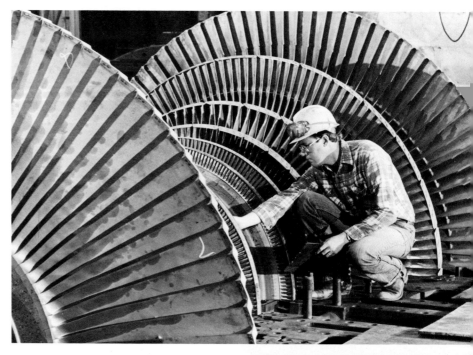

At CEI's Eastlake Plant, technical engineer Jeff Griggs inspects turbine blades during a recent plant maintenance project.

tract more than 900 companies to the area between 1945 and 1986.

Faced with rising electricity consumption, CEI in 1954 added the Eastlake Plant to its generating facilities. Today the plant has a generating capacity of 1,129 megawatts, making it the biggest producer among CEI's coal-fired power plants. The year that Eastlake came on line, the company's sales exceeded one billion kilowatt hours for the first time. In 1986 CEI sales reached nearly 18 billion kilowatt hours.

In 1974 CEI joined four other electric utilities to begin construction of the Perry Nuclear Power Plant to help meet future energy needs. Located in North Perry Village, the Perry Plant is the largest construction project in Ohio history. The plant received its operating license in 1986. Hundreds of Perry Plant workers are among the nearly 2,000 CEI employees who live in Lake County.

In completing the Perry Plant to help ensure the future energy secu-

At the Perry Plant, technician Julie Cunningham logs inspection reports into the computer. The reports are just one part of Perry's 12-year licensing process that has involved hundreds of technical experts.

rity of Northeast Ohio, CEI is acting on the tradition once defined by a former company chairman, Elmer L. Lindseth: "A public utility, more than any other type of company, is part of the people and area it serves. Such a company, therefore, has the responsibility of working—not only for itself—but for the development of the entire region that supports it."

PATRONS

The following individuals, companies, and organizations have made a valuable commitment to the quality of this publication. Windsor Publications and the Lake County Historical Society gratefully acknowledge their participation in *Lake County, Ohio: 150 Years of Tradition.*

Avery International (Fasson)*
Dr. and Mrs. Jack Battersby
Champion Marketing Co.
The Cleveland Electric Illuminating Company*
The Coe Manufacturing Company*
Davis Funeral Home*
Euclid Fish Company
Lake Hospital System, Inc.*
Jerry and Jeff Long
Dr. J.T. McCann
Madison Historical Society
Mentor Lumber and Supply Company*
Northeastern Ohio General Hospital*
Ohio Broach & Machine Company*
Ohio Rubber Company*
Perfection Corporation*
Quail Hollow Resort*
Talbot Insurance Agency
Teledyne Oster*
Transcon Incorporated*
WISCO Piston Inc.

*Partners in Progress of *Lake County, Ohio: 150 Years of Tradition.* The histories of these companies and organizations appear in Chapter 7, beginning on page 103.

BIBLIOGRAPHY

INSTITUTIONS FOR RESEARCH

Fairport Harbor Historical Society at the Fairport Marine Museum. FHHS.
Fairport Public Library. FPL.
Geauga County Public Library. GCPL.
Holden Arboretum. HA.
Lake County Historical Society. LCHS.
Lake County Indian Museum. LCIM.
Lake Erie College Archives. LECA.
Lake Metroparks. LM.
Madison Historical Society. MHS.
Morley Library, Painesville. ML.
Western Reserve Historical Society. WRHS.
Willoughby Historical Society. WHS.
Willoughby Public Library. WPL.

NEWSPAPERS FOR RESEARCH

Cleveland *Plain Dealer.* WRHS.
Geauga *Democrat.* GCPL.
Geauga *Times Leader.* GCPL, WRHS.
Madison Press. MHS.
Painesville *Telegraph.* LCHS, ML, WRHS.
Willoughby *Independent.* WPL.
Willoughby *News-Herald.* WPL.
Willoughby *Republican.* WPL.

MANUSCRIPT COLLECTIONS

Cleveland. Western Reserve Historical Society. John M. Henderson Papers, 1818-1850. MS 533.
Cleveland. Western Reserve Historical Society. Manuscripts Relating to the Early History of the Connecticut Western Reserve, 1795-1860. MS 1.
Cleveland. Western Reserve Historical Society. Dr. John Mathews Papers. MS 3891.
Cleveland. Western Reserve Historical Society. Samuel Mathews Papers, 1849-1909. 85-108MS.
Cleveland. Western Reserve Historical Society. Hendrick E. Pain Family Papers, 1788-1941. MS 3492.
Cleveland. Western Reserve Historical Society. Abraham Skinner Papers, 1786-1857. MS 1270.
Cleveland. Western Reserve Historical Society. Jeptha Wade Family Papers, 1837-1925. MS 3292.
Cleveland. Western Reserve Historical

Society. Willoughby, Ohio, Records, 1815-1874. MS 91.
Cleveland. Western Reserve Historical Society. Willoughby University of Lake Erie, Chagrin, Ohio. Records, 1834-1847. MS 2352.
Fairport Harbor. Fairport Harbor Historical Society. Abraham Skinner Papers.
Kirtland Hills. Lake County Historical Society. Nelson Slater. "Advertisement and Description of Western Reserve Teacher's Seminary and Kirtland Institute." Painesville, Ohio: Steele's Press, 25 July 1838.
Painesville. Lake Erie College Archives. Luette P. Bentley Papers.
Painesville. Lake Erie College Archives. Clippings Book, 1888-1897.
Painesville. Lake Erie College Archives. Clippings Book, 1901-1906.
Painesville. Lake Erie College Archives. Mary A. Evans Papers.
Willoughby. Willoughby Historical Society. Clippings Books.
Willoughby. Willoughby Historical Society. Sadie Talbot Eddy Diaries.

PRIMARY SOURCES

Annual Catalogues of the Lake Erie Female Seminary in Painesville, Ohio. 1859-1897. Painesville: Telegraph Job Office.
Annual Catalogues of Lake Erie College. 1898-1929. Painesville: Telegraph Job Office.
Annual Catalogues of the Willoughby Female Seminary, Willoughby, Lake County, Ohio. 1848-1855. Cleveland: McYounglove and Company.
Crary, Christopher Gore. *Pioneer and Personal Reminiscences.* Marshalltown, Iowa: Marshall Printing Co., 1893.
Evans, Mary A. *A Book of Friendship: Two Episodes in the Friendly Life,* Cedar Rapids, Iowa: Torch Press, 1925.
Ferriss, E.J. *History of Little Mountain from 1810-1887.* Painesville: Painesville Advertiser, 1887.
Fiftieth Anniversary of Lake Erie College, Painesville, Ohio, June 20-24, 1909. Cleveland: Alumnae Association, 1910.

Howe, Eber D. *Autobiography and Recollections of a Pioneer Printer.* Painesville: Telegraph Steam Printing House, 1878.
———. *Mormonism Unvailed.* Painesville: E.D. Howe, 1834.
Kirtland, Turhand. *Diary of Turhand Kirtland from 1798-1800.* Poland, Ohio, 1903.
Lake Erie Record. September/October 1898-June 1929. Painesville, Ohio: Lake Erie College.
"Lake Erie Seminary Journal." 7 September 1859-February 1875. (Typescript).
"Seminary Recorder." December 1891-June 1898. (Typescript).
Twenty-Fifth Anniversary of Lake Erie Female Seminary Painesville, Ohio June 23-26, 1884. Cleveland: J.B. Savage, 1885.

SECONDARY SOURCES— ARTICLES, ESSAYS, AND REPORTS

Andrews, Alice. "Visiting a Realm of Cleveland Aristocracy: Since 1816 the Pine-Clad Crest of Little Mountain Out Beyond Willoughby Has Been a Haven for Many Prominent Families." *Cleveland Plain Dealer Magazine,* 27 November 1932. WRHS. Microfilm.
Anker, Daniel. "Lessons from Erie Warfare." *Western Reserve Studies* 1 (1986): 9-12.
Bellows, Cynthia. "Little Mountain." *Western Reserve Magazine,* Special Supplement, October 1981, p. 76.
Brose, David. "History as a Handmaiden to Archaeology?" *Ohio Archaeologist* 34, No. 1 (Winter 1984): 28-30.
Brown, Harry James. "As the Twig is Bent: The Education of the Garfield Children." *Lake County Historical Society Quarterly* 23, No. 1 (March 1981).
Brown, Jeffrey P. "Samuel Huntington: A Connecticut Aristocrat on the Ohio Frontier." *Ohio History* 89, No. 4 (Autumn 1980): 420-438.
Bush, David R. "The Erie Indians and the Whittlesey Focus: Late Aboriginal Life in Northeastern Ohio." *Lake County Historical Society Quarterly* 26, No. 4 (December 1984).
Bush, David R., and Callander, Charles. "Anybody But the Erie." *Ohio Archaeologist* 34,

No. 1 (Winter 1984): 31-35.

Cardinal, Jare R. and Eric J. "Archaeology and History: Some Suggestion from the Historians Point of View." *Ohio Archaeologist* 34, No. 2 (Spring 1984): 34-38.

Catanzaro, James L. *President's Report, Lakeland: The First Two Decades.* Mentor, Ohio: Lakeland Community College (1987).

Demerson, George, comp. *Perry's Victory Centenary: Report of the Perry Victory Centennial Commission, State of New York.* Albany: J.B. Lyon Co. Printers, 1916.

Edwards, Linden F. "Body Snatching in Ohio During the Nineteenth Century." *The Ohio State Archaeological and Historical Quarterly* LIX (1950).

Gamble, Douglas A. "Joshua Giddings and the Ohio Abolitionists: A Study in Radical Politics." *Ohio History* 88, No. 1 (Winter 1979): 37-56.

Goulder, Grace. "Ohio Scenes and Citizens: Little Mountain, Once Famed for Hotel and 'Hygenic Air', is now Taken Over by Big Estates." *Cleveland Plain Dealer Magazine,* 22 May 1949. WRHS. Microfilm.

Grant, H. Roger. "Interurban!" *Timeline,* April/May 1986, pp. 14-33.

Green, Jerie Ireland. "A Mansion for Mentor." *Western Reserve Magazine,* September/October 1980, pp. 32-33.

Greenman, Emerson F. "Excavation of the Reeve Village Site, Lake County, Ohio." *Ohio State Archaeological and Historical Quarterly* 44, No. 2 (April 1935): 6-21.

————. "Seven Prehistorical Sites in Northern Ohio." *Ohio State Archaeological and Historical Quarterly* 44, No. 2 (April 1935).

Haddad, Gladys. "The Ladies of Lake Erie College." *Western Reserve Magazine,* November/December 1981, pp. 49-53.

Hays, Deborah. "Fairport's Guiding Light." *Western Reserve Magazine,* March/April 1976, pp. 18-19.

Holden Arboretum. "Holden Arboretum . . . A Brief History." Promotional Brochure, 1985.

"House For Sale: It's Ohio's Only Five-Hundred-Year-Old Home, A Genuine Fifteenth-Century English Manor House." *Western Reserve Magazine,* December 1985/January 1986, pp. 62-63.

Long, Byron R. "Joseph Badger, The First Missionary to the Western Reserve." *Ohio Archaeological and Historical Publication* XXVI.

Lupold, Harry Forrest. "Ben Wade: The Practical Radical." *Western Reserve Magazine,* November/December 1980, pp. 65-67.

————. "Josh Giddings: Champion of Human Rights." *Western Reserve Magazine,* November/December 1980, pp. 62-65.

Marcus, Robert D. "James A. Garfield: Lifting the Mask." *Ohio History* (Winter 1979): 78-83.

McNiff, W.J. "The Kirtland Phase of Mormonism." *The Ohio State Archaeological and Historical Quarterly* L (July-September 1941).

Miller, Carolyn. "Neighbors: Lore of Lake County, Ohio." *New York Folklore Quarterly* 6, No. 3 (Autumn 1950): 168-194.

Mills, William S. "Lake County and its Founder." *Ohio Archaeological and Historical Publications* X (1902).

Morgan, Richard G., and Ellis, Homer H. "The Fairport Harbor Village Site." *Ohio State Archaeological and Historical Quarterly* 52, No. 1. (January-March 1943): 3-64.

Norris, James D., and Martin, James K., eds. "Three Civil War Letters of James A. Garfield." *Ohio History* 74, No. 4 (Autumn 1965): 247-252.

Palmer, Louisa Velnett. "Lincoln of the Western Reserve." *Western Reserve Magazine,* September/October 1980, pp. 48-49.

Peskin, Allan. "The Hero of Sandy Valley: James A. Garfield's Kentucky Campaign of 1861-1862." *Ohio History* 72, No. 1 (January 1963): 3-24.

————. "The Hero of Sandy Valley: James A. Garfield's Kentucky Campaign of 1861-1862 - II." *Ohio History* 72, No. 2 (April 1963): 129-139.

————. "The Western Reserve's Favorite Son." *Western Reserve Magazine,* September/October 1980, pp. 39-47.

Prusha, Anne. "Early Education in Kirtland, 1803-1920." *Western Reserve Magazine,* March/April 1983, pp. 30-32.

Ross, A.I. "Ohio's Great Five Cent Ride." *Western Reserve Magazine* Vol. VIII, No. 7, pp. 20-23.

Scharf, Lois. "Helpmates and Housewives: Women's Changing Roles in the Western Reserve, 1800-1870." *Western Reserve Magazine,* Vol. 5, No. 4 (May/June 1979).

Shriver, Phillip R. "The Beaver Wars and the Destruction of the Erie Nation." *Timeline,* December 1984/January 1985, pp. 29-41.

Southworth, Elizabeth. "Days of the Lake Shore Electric." *Western Reserve Magazine,* Vol. VIII, No. 7, pp. 24-26.

Stith, Bari. "'Blest Be the Tie That Binds': Mary Evans, 'True Education,' and the Young Ladies of the Lake Erie Female Seminary, 1869-1909." *Journal of the Midwest History of Education Society* 15 (1987): 205-214.

————. "Keeper of the Flame: Mary Evans and Her Impact on Lake Erie Female Seminary." *Lake County Historical Quarterly* 27, No's. 3 & 4 (September/December 1985): 25-28.

Theis, Jana M. "Indian Museum." *Western Reserve Magazine,* September/October 1981, pp. 65-67.

————. "Lake County Historical Society Finds a New Home." *Western Reserve Magazine,* December 1984/January 1985, pp. 34-27.

Thompson, Jack M. "James R. Garfield: The Making of a Progressive." *Ohio History* 74, No. 2 (Spring 1965): 79-89.

Thornton, Willis. "Gentile and Saint and Kirtland." *Ohio State Archaeological and Historical Quarterly* 63, No. 1 (January 1954): 8-33.

Wheeler, Robert A. "Shakers and Mormons in the Early Western Reserve: A Contrast in Lifestyles." *Western Reserve Magazine,* July-August 1978, pp. 27-34.

Wheeler, Robert A. "Water to Steam: Industry in the Western Reserve, 1800-1860." *Western Reserve Magazine,* September/October 1978, pp. 27-34.

White, Marian E. "Erie." *Handbook of North American Indians* Vol. 15. Bruce G. Trigger, ed. Washington: Smithsonian Institution.

"Willoughby's Little Red Schoolhouse." *Western Reserve Magazine,* September/October, 1978, pp. 16-17.

SECONDARY SOURCES—BOOKS AND PAMPHLETS

A Memoir of Rev. Joseph Badger. Hudson, Ohio: Sawyer, Ingersoll and Co., 1851.

Annals of Cleveland 1818-1935: Abstracts from the Daily True Democrat. Cleveland: WPA Project, 1938.

Atlas of Lake and Geauga Counties, Ohio. Philadelphia: Titus, Simmons and Titus, 1874.

Atlas of Lake County, Ohio. Cleveland: H.B. Stranahan and Co., 1898.

The Bicentennial Edition of Lake County History. Painesville: Lake County Historical Society and Board of Lake County Commissioners, 1976.

Brodie, Fawn M. *No Man Knows My History.* New York: Alfred A. Knopf, 1945.

Butler, Margaret Manor. *A Pictorial History of the Western Reserve, 1796-1860.* Cleveland: The Early Settlers Association of the Western Reserve and the Western Reserve Historical Society, 1963.

Card, Jonathan Ford. *The Life of Jonathan Ford Card.* Cleveland: J.B. Savage, 1897.

Cherry, P.P. *The Western Reserve and Early Ohio.* Akron: R.L. Fouse, 1921.

Downes, Randolph C. *History of Lake Shore Ohio.* 3 vols. New York: Lewis Historical Publishing Co., 1952.

Eggleston, Margaret W., ed. *Kathie's Diary.* New York: George Doran, 1926.

Folger, Will R.; Folger, Mary H.; and Lupold, Harry Forrest. *The Western Reserve Story.* Garrettsville, Ohio: Western Reserve Magazine, 1981.

Gault, Homer J., ed. *History of Mentor Headlands and Vicinity.* Fairport Harbor: North Mentor Service Circle, 1957.

Geauga and Lake County Genealogical Society, comp. *1857 Landowners' Map of Geauga and Lake Counties, Ohio, Indexed.* 1985.

Geauga County Historical and Memorial Society. *Pioneer and General History of Geauga County.* Columbus: Stoneman Press, 1953.

Griffen, Jane G., ed. *Here Is Lake County, Ohio.* Cleveland: Howard Allen, Inc., Pub., 1964.

Hatcher, Harlan. *Lake Erie.* Indianapolis: Bobbs Merrill Co., Inc., 1945.

————. *The Western Reserve: The Story of New Connecticut in Ohio.* Indianapolis: Bobbs Merrill Co. Inc., 1949.

Henninge, Rose. *A Sociological Study of the Village of Fairport Harbor, Ohio.* (By the Author, 1956).

Hillis, L.B., ed. *Lake County Illustrated 1912: Historical, Biographical and Statistical, The County as it is Today.* Painesville: The Herald Printing Company, 1912.

History of Geauga and Lake Counties: With Illustrations and Biographical Sketches of Its Pioneers and Most Prominent Men. Philadelphia: Williams Brothers, 1878.

Howe, Henry. *Historical Collection of Ohio.* 3 vols. Cincinnati: E. Morgan and Co., 1861.

————. *Historical Collections of Ohio.* 2 vols. Columbus: The State of Ohio, 1888.

Kolehmainen, John I. *From Lake Erie's Shores to the Mahoning and Monongahela Valleys: A History of the Finns in Ohio, Western Pennsylvania and West Virginia.* New York Mills, Minnesota: Parta Printers, Inc. for the Ohio-Finnish American Historical Society, 1977.

Koryta, Rose C. *The Growth of Wickliffe, Ohio.* Wickliffe Public Library, 1967.

Lafferty, Michael, ed. *Ohio's Natural Heritage.* Columbus: Ohio Academy of Science, 1979.

Lake County Heritage. LCHS Pamphlet.

Lindsey, David. *Ohio's Western Reserve: The Story of Its Place Names.* Cleveland: Western Reserve University Press, 1955.

Lottich, Kenneth V. *New England Transplanted.* Dallas: Royal Publishing Co., 1964.

Lupold, Harry Forrest. *Forgotten People: The Woodland Erie.* Hicksville, New York: Exposition Press, 1975.

————. *The Latch String Is Out: A Pioneer History of Lake County, Ohio.* Mentor, Ohio: Lakeland Community College Press, 1974.

Merrell, Fred E., ed. *Lake County Observes Ohio's Sesquicentennial, 1803-1953.* Painesville: Educational Supply Co., 1953.

Natural History of Lake County. LCHS Pamphlet.

New Century Atlas: Lake County, Ohio. Philadelphia: Century Map Co., 1915.

Ohio's Writers' Project. *Lake County History.* Cleveland: Western Reserve Historical Society, Lake County Chapter, 1941.

Old Mentor Foundation. *The Architecture of Mentor, Ohio: A Guide to Historic Buildings.* Mentor: Old Mentor Foundation in association with Lakeland Community College, 1973.

Olin, Saul. *Hometown Sketches.* Fairport: Saul Olin, 1936.

————, ed. *The Story of Fairport, Ohio.* Fairport, 1946.

Peskin, Allan. *Garfield.* Kent State University Press, 1978.

Potter, Martha. *Ohio's Prehistoric Peoples.* Columbus: Ohio Historical Society, 1968.

Prusha, Anne B. *A History of Kirtland, Ohio.* Mentor, Ohio: Lakeland Community College Press, 1982.

Rice, Harvey. *Incidents of Pioneer Life in the Early Settlement of the Connecticut Western Reserve.* Cleveland: Cobb, Andrews and Co., 1881.

————. *Pioneers of the Western Reserve.* Boston: Lee and Shephard Publisher, 1883.

Rose, William Ganson. *Cleveland: The Making of a City.* Cleveland: World Press, 1950.

Shankland, Frank N. *Historical Willoughby.* Centennial Celebration, 1953.

Stewart, John S. *History of Northeastern Ohio.* 3 vols. Indianapolis: Historical Publishing Company, 1935.

Swain, Sandra A. *By the Buckeye: A Complete History of the Village/Center Street School Plus an Overview of the History of Mentor and All of Its Schools.* Center Street School Parent Teacher Club, 1984.

Upton, Harriet Taylor. *A History of the Western Reserve.* 3 vols. Chicago: The Lewis Publishing Co., 1910.

Vietzen, Raymond C. *Indians of the Lake Erie Basin, or Lost Nations.* By the Author, 1965.

————. *The Immortal Eries.* Elyria, Ohio, 1945.

Waite, Frederick Crawford. *An Historical Sketch of the Willoughby Medical College, 1834-1847.* Cleveland: Western Reserve University, (ca. 1930s).

————. *Place Names in Lake County and Vicinity.* 1939.

Wallace, Marie. *Come to the Country: The Story of Balla Machree.* Cleveland: World Publishing Company, 1953.

Whittlesey, Charles. *Early History of Cleveland, Ohio.* Cleveland: Fairbanks, Benedict and Co., 1867.

Wickham, Gertrude Van Rensselaer, ed. *Memorial to the Pioneer Women of the Western Reserve.* 3 vols. Cleveland: Women's Department of the Cleveland Centennial Commission, 1896.

Workers of the Writers' Program. *Lake County Landmarks.* Columbus, Ohio: Ohio State Archaeological and Historical Society, 1940.

SECONDARY SOURCES— UNPUBLISHED MATERIALS

"The Celebration, Silver Anniversary of the Lake Metroparks." 1983. (Typewritten.) LM.

Cooper, B.J., comp. "New Market." 1959. (Typewritten.) WHS.

Goldstein, Linda Lenmann. "A Closer Look at the Water Cure: Choices for Women in the American Popular Health Reform Movement in Antebellum America." Paper presented at the 20th Annual Buquesne History Forum, Pittsburgh, Pennsylvania, 29 October 1986.

Haddad, Gladys. "Social Roles and Advanced Education for Women in Nineteenth Century America: A Study of Three Western Reserve Institutions." Ph.D. Dissertation, Case Western Reserve University, 1980.

Kasari, Helen. "Ralph Granger, A Pioneer of Fairport." Paper presented to the Lake County Genealogical Society, Painesville, Ohio, 19 November 1980. FHHS.

"Metroparks Background." 1986. (Typewritten.) LM.

Stith, Bari Oyler. "A Treasured Place: The Changing Community of Little Mountain." (Typewritten.)

Stith, Bari Oyler. "Blest Be the Tie That Binds: Mary Evans, 'True Education,' and the Young Ladies of the Lake Erie Female Seminary." M.A. Thesis, Case Western Reserve University, 1986.

INDEX